FIGURES AROUND THE CROSS

Figures Around the Cross
A Lenten Journey From Death To Life

Reverend William F. Maestri

ALBA·HOUSE   alba house   NEW·YORK

SOCIETY OF ST. PAUL, 2187 VICTORY BLVD., STATEN ISLAND, NEW YORK 10314

ST PAULS

Library of Congress Cataloging-in-Publication Data

Maestri, William.
    Figures around the Cross: A Lenten journey from death to life / by William F. Maestri.
        p. cm.
    ISBN 0-8189-0909-9 (alk. paper)
    1. Lent—Prayer-books and devotions—English. 2. Catholic Church—Prayer-books and devotions—English. 3. Bible. N.T. Gospels—Devotional literature. I. Title.

    BX2170.L4 M24 2002
    242'.34—dc21

                                                    2001046228

Nihil Obstat:
Reverend Dennis J. Hayes, III
Censor Librorum

Imprimatur:
✠ Most Reverend Francis B. Schulte
Archbishop of New Orleans
May 28, 2001

The Nihil Obstat and Imprimatur are a declaration that a book or pamphlet is considered to be free from doctrinal or moral error. It is not implied that those who have granted the Nihil Obstat and Imprimatur agree with the contents, opinions or statements expressed.

Produced and designed in the United States of America by the Fathers and Brothers of the Society of St. Paul, 2187 Victory Boulevard, Staten Island, New York 10314-6603, as part of their communications apostolate.

ISBN: 0-8189-0909-9

Printing Information:

Current Printing - first digit	1	2	3	4	5	6	7	8	9	10

Year of Current Printing - first year shown

2002	2003	2004	2005	2006	2007	2008	2009	2010

DEDICATION

*In appreciation to all
at Our Lady of Malibu
and Pepperdine Law School
for making a stranger welcomed.*

Table of Contents

V. FIGURES AROUND THE CROSS

VI. EASTER AND EMMAUS

Introduction

In my Advent and Christmas book, *Figures Around The Crib*, I began by asking a simple question. Why does this crib continue to draw us into its presence? The answer was simple (hopefully not simplistic) LOVE. The crib reveals the great mystery of the union between the divine and the human. The God who dwells in unapproachable light takes on a human face in Jesus. The Logos becomes flesh and dwells among us (Jn 1:14). The Holy Family is also a very human family required to face the challenges of raising a child in difficult circumstances.

As we turn our attention to Lent and Easter, we must ask anew. Why does the cross continue to draw us into its presence? This previously asked question elicits a familiar reply, LOVE. Yet unlike the crib, the association of the cross with love is at once theologically challenging and spiritually demanding.

The very idea of a Suffering Messiah who would be rejected and put to death has always proven theologically troubling. The Messiah *we* desire is triumphant and subjects all principalities and powers under his reign. The notion of a Messiah who takes up the cross is a scandal, folly, a stumbling block, and a counter-sign which shows weakness rather than strength (1 Cor 1:18-25). However, the Messiah of *God* is one who heals by his wounds (Is 53:5); dies our death so that we might have life, and rises on the third day as our hope of glory (Col 1:27). God is love; and the depth of the divine love is revealed on the cross (1 Jn 4:7-10).

The spirituality of the cross reveals the costly grace of discipleship. The cross teaches a spiritual *realism* which must confront the hostility of the world (Jn 15:18-27). The world is under the influence of the powers of darkness and the Father of Lies. The Light who is Truth shines in the darkness of sin. This only serves to increase the violence of the world toward Jesus *and* those who are his witnesses (martyrs). There is no offer of a cheap grace which comes packaged in pietistic romanticism. In the words of Dietrich Bonhoeffer, "When Jesus calls a man he bids him to come and die." At the same time, the invitation to die is the offer of new life. The realism of the cross does not end in despair but in the patient hope of resurrection. In the midst of the world's hostility, Jesus proclaims, "...my peace is my gift to you... be not afraid... Take courage! I have overcome the world" (Jn 14:27; 16:33).

The shadow of the cross is long and deep, extending the length of human history and plummeting to the core of human nature. Soon after creation, the serpent appears in the garden. In short order, humankind rebels against the Creator of heaven and earth. Sin disfigures the human heart and all of nature as well. If pride goes before the Fall, banishment follows and human history unfolds east of Eden. We can't go home again. Yet even in the midst of the alienation and chaos which results from sin, the message of hope is planted beneath the soil (Gn 3:15; Rm 2:6-7). In the words of the Fourth Eucharistic Prayer, "Even when he disobeyed you and lost your friendship, you did not abandon him to the power of death.... Again and again you offered a covenant to man."

While Golgotha contains the definitive expression of the cross, its formation began in Eden and will continue into eternity. Easter-faith cannot be separated from Good Friday's suffering-love. Easter-hope is real and never forgets the costs of this tremendous love. In the days after the resurrection, Jesus appears to the Eleven on several occasions. The resurrected Jesus carries the marks of the crucifixion. They serve as an eternal reminder of the cost of sin and the greater effect of love following upon love (Jn 1:16). Such a love is easy to doubt. Like Thomas, we condition our belief on "probing the nailprints in his hands" and putting our "hand into his side" (Jn 20:25). Lent is the acceptable time for passing from unbelief to belief. In so doing, the words of Jesus will be for us, "Blest are they who have not seen and have believed" (Jn 20:29).

During the season of Lent, the Church calls us to that journey in belief from death to life. Such a passage requires a willingness to take up our cross daily and be one with Jesus on the way to Jerusalem (Lk 9:23-27). In spite of its natural repugnance with its violence, abuse, and degradation, to the eye of faith, it is "the power of God and the wisdom of God" (1 Cor 1:24). Along with the Eucharist, private prayer, and the works of charity, the daily teaching of Scripture is indispensable for our passage to Jerusalem. For we do not want merely to be a figure around the cross, we want to be born anew by the Spirit given by Jesus (Jn 19:30). We want to become members of that family born in the shadow of the cross. We want to be one with Mary and the disciple whom Jesus loved (Jn 19:25-27).

The format of this book is simple. For each day of Lent, the reader is offered a selection from Scripture along with a reflection to help one's journey to Jerusalem. In addition, there is a brief prayer and a series of questions for personal reflection. The completion of Lent is a commencement into Easter *and beyond*. While the cross leads to the empty tomb, the story of Easter must *continue* to be told as the Church unfolds down the road to Emmaus.

I wish to express my gratitude to Father Edmund Lane, SSP and the entire Society of Saint Paul community of ALBA HOUSE at Staten Island. Your ministry of evangelization through various forms of print media and telecommunications is crucial in the third millennium. The work of Saint Paul continues. I am grateful to contribute to this ministry with the writing of this book.

May God's grace make up what is lacking in these pages.

May this book be a source of inspiration to all who journey to Jerusalem, gather around the cross, and live each day proclaiming, "He has been raised from the dead…" (Mt 28:6).

William F. Maestri
Our Lady of Malibu Catholic Church
Malibu, California
Lent-Easter, 2002

May I never boast of anything
but the cross of our Lord Jesus Christ!
Through it, the world
has been crucified to me
and I to the world.
(Gal 6:14)

Biblical Abbreviations

OLD TESTAMENT

Genesis	Gn	Nehemiah	Ne	Baruch	Ba
Exodus	Ex	Tobit	Tb	Ezekiel	Ezk
Leviticus	Lv	Judith	Jdt	Daniel	Dn
Numbers	Nb	Esther	Est	Hosea	Ho
Deuteronomy	Dt	1 Maccabees	1 M	Joel	Jl
Joshua	Jos	2 Maccabees	2 M	Amos	Am
Judges	Jg	Job	Jb	Obadiah	Ob
Ruth	Rt	Psalms	Ps	Jonah	Jon
1 Samuel	1 S	Proverbs	Pr	Micah	Mi
2 Samuel	2 S	Ecclesiastes	Ec	Nahum	Na
1 Kings	1 K	Song of Songs	Sg	Habakkuk	Hab
2 Kings	2 K	Wisdom	Ws	Zephaniah	Zp
1 Chronicles	1 Ch	Sirach	Si	Haggai	Hg
2 Chronicles	2 Ch	Isaiah	Is	Malachi	Ml
Ezra	Ezr	Jeremiah	Jr	Zechariah	Zc
		Lamentations	Lm		

NEW TESTAMENT

Matthew	Mt	Ephesians	Eph	Hebrews	Heb
Mark	Mk	Philippians	Ph	James	Jm
Luke	Lk	Colossians	Col	1 Peter	1 P
John	Jn	1 Thessalonians	1 Th	2 Peter	2 P
Acts	Ac	2 Thessalonians	2 Th	1 John	1 Jn
Romans	Rm	1 Timothy	1 Tm	2 John	2 Jn
1 Corinthians	1 Cor	2 Timothy	2 Tm	3 John	3 Jn
2 Corinthians	2 Cor	Titus	Tt	Jude	Jude
Galatians	Gal	Philemon	Phm	Revelation	Rv

FIGURES AROUND THE CROSS

I

IN THE BEGINNING

To understand the meaning and truth of the cross, we must read history in reverse. We must advance to the beginning. The cross begins to take shape in Eden. Soon after creation sin enters the world. And with sin its wages—death. Although our first parents are banished, they are not abandoned. There is the promise of a redeemer. However, this promise will be realized only in the fullness of time. There is no "quick fix" to sin. There will be a long twilight struggle with the unfolding of God's plan. A new people must be chosen, not out of the dust of the earth but over the course of history. The God who creates is also the Lord of history. Both nature and history are rescued from futility by the God who *acts* in time to liberate, redeem, and recreate.

In this opening section, we explore the foundations of who we are and our relationship with the Creator of heaven and earth. Truth requires that we face the reality of sin and its enduring effects on human nature. At the same time, we must dare to hope in the promise of the One who is worthy of our trust. Again, we must acknowledge Israel's uneven response to Yahweh's self-disclosure. More importantly, we must acknowledge God's display of faithful love (*hesed*). Time and again God seeks the lost sheep of the house of Israel.

Before we begin our Lenten journey by revisiting Eden, we

must make an initial stop, brief but essential. We must start at Bethlehem, for the crib is that distant mirror which reflects the ever present reality of the cross, the cost of discipleship, and the depth of the Divine Love for us.

A Sign of Opposition

What a strange place to begin Lent!

Admittedly, Bethlehem is not the first place that comes to mind when we think of Lent. Bethlehem is associated with Advent and the birth of the Messiah. We have come to think of Advent and Christmas as the polar opposite of Lent and Easter. Bethlehem and Golgotha call for different approaches to discipleship. In Bethlehem the angel proclaims good news and glad tidings of great joy (Lk 2:10-11). On Golgotha Jesus "cried out in a loud voice, 'My God, my God, why have you forsaken me?'" (Mk 15:34). It would seem that each place has its separate part to play in salvation history. Yet, we must ask right at the start: While each has its place, are we to understand the Incarnation and the Paschal Mystery as distinct aspects of Jesus? The answer supplied by the Scriptures is NO. Bethlehem and Golgotha, crib and cross, Incarnation and Paschal Mystery, Advent-Christmas and Lent-Easter must be viewed holistically. That is, while we may speak about them separately in terms of analysis, in the life of Jesus they are complementary. We must view the Jesus-event in a total way so as to avoid an imbalance which distorts and can lead to a myopic vision of Jesus. Fidelity to the Scriptures and to the Catholic-thing requires that we start our Lent in Bethlehem.

BORN TO MIXED REVIEWS

The birth of a child is usually cause for celebration. Yet, we know there are times when the festivities are muted or even absent. The cause is not the child but the circumstances or the people involved. With the birth of Jesus, Scripture tells us there was a variety of reactions. And the reactions had to do with the birth of *this* child.

To be sure, there were manifestations of great joy and wonder—the astrologers from the east (Mt 2:1-12); the shepherds in the fields (Lk 2:8-18); a multitude of the heavenly host (Lk 2:13-14); Anna the prophetess (Lk 2:36-40); Simeon (Lk 2:22-32); and the parents of Jesus as well (Lk 2:33). This litany of joy at the birth of Jesus is both welcomed and familiar. It is of these reactions that the stuff of Advent and Christmas are made.

At the same time, there is a manifestation of opposition and deadly hostility toward this child. King Herod was greatly disturbed at the report of the birth of "the newborn king of the Jews" (Mt 2:1-4); Herod's hostility causes the Holy Family to flee into Egypt (Mt 2:13-15); the martyrdom of the Holy Innocents (Mt 2:16-18); and even the presentation of Jesus in the temple recounts the pious Simeon telling Mary that Jesus is "a sign that will be opposed" and even she will experience a piercing sword (Lk 2:33-35).

The nativity narratives by Matthew and Luke do not present us with a contrived uniformity of the event. There is a rich complexity which blends together in order to provide us with a rich spirituality. What emerges is a spirituality which strengthens our discipleship, sobers our expectations about Jesus, and reveals the cost that is to be paid by the One who comes to do the will of the Father (Jn 17:6-8).

Spiritual Realism

The nativity narratives refuse to be domesticated into nice stories about the season to be jolly. The stories of our commercial culture are at odds with the biblical realism of the birth of the Messiah. For the Word made flesh will become the Man of Sorrows; the child who is presented with gifts of gold, frankincense, and myrrh will in time be offered "a sponge soaked in sour wine on some hyssop" while he hangs on the cross (Mt 2:11; Jn 19:29). We know that the heavenly host who proclaim, "Glory to God in high heaven" will make room for a frenzied mob crying, "Crucify him! Crucify him!" (Lk 2:14; Jn 19:15). The peace proclaimed at Christmas can only be achieved through the baptism of fire on Good Friday. Matthew's nativity narrative is biblical realism at its best and most essential. The hostility and murderous intent of the world toward Jesus is present at the beginning. The One who comes offers life in abundance. The response of the world is violence and death (Jn 15:18-21).

The desire to prevent Jesus from going to Jerusalem is not new. We are attracted to a Christ without a cross. But such a Messiah does not have the power to conquer sin and death. The hard realism of Lent, with its costly grace, is this: "If anyone wishes to come after me, he must deny his very self, take up his cross, and begin to follow in my footsteps" (Mt 16:24). To the natural eye, such an invitation leads to death. To the eye of faith, Jesus is offering the way to eternal help. The decision is ours. The time is now.

As with all journeys, especially the journey of faith, we must begin at the beginning. It is on to Eden....

PRAYER

O Lord, we find ourselves at the beginning of a
new season of Lent.
The ashes are still visible. The firm purpose of
amending our sinful ways is strong. We
want to change. We want to turn from sin
and all that keeps us from loving you.

Yet, you know we are weak. We are dust. We are
but a breath in time. The vessel of clay that
we are, easily grows brittle and breaks. O Lord,

we need your life-breath to renew our
drooping spirit and strengthen our resolve.

O Lord, you invite us to follow you. Yet, we
know the cost is great. Cheap grace will
not sustain us on the way to Jerusalem. We
must deny our very selves and daily
pick up our cross. But can we do such a
thing? Can we accept such an invitation?
Can we carry such a burden?

Loving Father, by ourselves we can do nothing.
We falter. Fear grips our hearts. Doubts
assail our resolve. We want to turn back.
It is at such moments your Son comes to
us with the words, "Follow me." He tells us
to "be not afraid." He will sustain us on
the journey. He will revive our spirits.
Jesus give us courage.

Reflection Questions

1. In what specific ways do you plan on participating in Lent?
   How will these various spiritual activities help you grow
   closer to Jesus?
2. What are some of the major obstacles that you experience
   in entering into the season of Lent? In what ways do you
   intend to overcome these obstacles?
3. How do you plan on growing in knowledge of the word
   of God? In what ways has the Bible been a source of spiritual strength to you? What are some obstacles you experience in reading the Scriptures? How might you overcome
   these obstacles?

Anatomy of a Fall

At last, we are on familiar ground. Eden and the Fall have a genuine Lenten ring to them, like sackcloth and ashes. After all, our fall from grace began in the Garden. In the midst of that first garden party came the serpent with its promise of God-like powers. The dust of the earth was no match for the glitter of the forbidden fruit. Why be a creature when being a creator is but a grasp away? Yet the reach exceeds the grasp; in consuming the forbidden fruit, they are consumed by their guilt and shame; and the innocent walks with God in the Garden are no more. Now our first parents hide themselves at the sound of Yahweh's call. There is a fearful vulnerability which comes from being naked. They are overfed on their pride and undernourished in the ways of the Lord. Their eyes are opened to know good and evil. But such knowledge is not meant for them. They must leave, never to return. An angel guards the way back. Human history will unfold east of Eden. Looking backward is futile as the image of the Garden becomes smaller in our nostalgia-covered rear-view mirror. It is only by going forward in hope that the earliest outline of the Kingdom begins to take shape on the horizon.

Such is the skeletal anatomy of the Fall. But bones are lifeless. Form requires matter; flesh and blood must be added if the human is to come forth. Even the Word becomes flesh (Jn 1:14). And so it is in the details of the human, all too human, that we must view the Fall. For in the details, we find the power of the serpent.

The stage for the Fall is set with the arrival of the serpent, "the most cunning of all the animals" (Gn 3:1). The temptation to rebellion is not a frontal assault on God but a rear-action maneuver. God is not directly rebuked but the *reasonableness* of his command is questioned. "Did God really tell you not to eat from any of the trees in the garden?" (Gn 3:1). The tactic is at once clever and effective. Such a limitation would lead to death. God is not only unreasonable; he is also murderous! No reasonable person would follow such a command. No truly good God would expect obedience. Disobedience becomes a duty.

The effect of the serpent's question is twofold: doubt and exaggeration. The total trust of Adam and Eve in the truth and goodness of God *may* be misplaced. For the first time, the irritation of doubt now enters. Maybe, just maybe, the God they serve is concerned only with preserving his power. If this is the case, then obedience to this tyrannical God is to contribute to immorality.

Once the seed of doubt is planted, it quickly yields the bitter fruit of exaggeration. Truth is no longer viewed as potent enough to expose a lie. We must inflate in order to quiet the doubt. However, the serpent has opened the door and one exaggeration is matched by another. Eve sets the record straight by half. Unfortunately, it is the *whole* truth which conquers the Father of Lies. So Eve feels the need to quote God's prohibition in the following way. "God said, 'You shall not eat it or even touch it, lest you die'" (Gn 3:3). Upon closer inspection, we see that God said nothing about "even touch it." None of this really matters. What is crucial is the dynamic set in motion by the serpent, doubt joined with exaggeration undermines trust. Perhaps disobedience will not lead to death but a new birth of freedom and power. It has such a modern ring. We only become mature to the extent we reject limits. Freedom comes from being our own law. We grasp at any tree which seems to open our eyes. Yet, in the end, there is a fall from grace which mars our humanity. Responsibility is avoided by blaming others. The tragic end is banishment. The fruit, pleasing to the eye, yields death not life (Gn 3:24).

Felix Culpa

There is no denying that this episode in humankind's history ends on an ominous note: "…he stationed the cherubim and the fiery revolving sword, to guard the way to the tree of life" (Gn 3:24). Yet, if there is a hint of the cross in Bethlehem, we can hear a rumor of the coming crib in the bleakness of Eden. "He will strike at your head, while you strike at his heel" (Gn 3:15). The works of the serpent will continue beyond the Garden. The serpent will follow humankind down the long road of history. Its works are as evident as they are numerous. However, the serpent will not gain the ultimate victory. For God is also present and active in history. In the fullness of time, the Word will become human in history so "that he might destroy the works of the devil" (1 Jn 3:8). How will he do this? In the words of the Pauline hymn in Philippians, "he… did not regard equality with God something to be grasped… he humbled himself, becoming obedient to death, even death on a cross. Because of this, God greatly exalted him…" (Ph 2:5-11).

If we listen carefully, we hear the faint chant of, "Felix culpa!", "Oh, happy fault!" But that is in the future. For now, we must learn to live east of Eden.

Prayer

O Lord, your creative word of love brings all
things into existence.
You order all things to their true end. Apart
from you there is no life.
The greatness of your creative love is found in

the being of the one who is made in
your image and likeness. For it is
only the one made of dust who is filled with
your life-breath.
At the coming into existence of the one made
in your image, you proclaim creation "very good."

O Lord, you love us so much you risk everything
by giving us freedom. For you want us to
love you as you love us. The love you want from
us is not commanded but must be offered as a
response to the love you first showed us.
Yet, we misuse that freedom. We
believe more in the love of power than in the
power of your love.

O Lord, we sin. We fail to trust in your
promises. We seek security in that which
glitters and seems to offer immortality. In
truth we fall. We are banished.

Yet, you do not abandon us. Your faithful love
will seek us out and call us home.
Not to a Garden but to your Kingdom of Light, Life, and Truth.

Reflection Questions

1. In what ways have you experienced God's creative love? How have you helped others become aware of God's love? How do you use your gifts for the common good?
2. How have you been tempted to abuse the gift of freedom? Have you given in to such temptations? How have you overcome various temptations?
3. Why do we human beings find it so difficult to trust? What specific aspects keep you from trusting God's promises? How have you been challenged to trust God's love within the past year? Did you accept the challenge? Why? Why not?

East of Eden

Freedom is always an experiment. To be conceived in liberty does not guarantee that the live birth of freedom will occur. There is always a price to pay. With greater freedom comes increased responsibility. Greater freedom increases the greater probability of lawlessness. The result of any risk with freedom depends greatly on the character of the individual and the makeup of the community.

History, as well as our personal experience, teaches that experiments in freedom can end with tragic results. Liberty can degenerate into a license that becomes self-indulgent and arrogant with power. The story of Eden is a profound episode in humankind's experiment with freedom. And God's experiment with freedom as well. Admittedly the initial results leave a great deal to be desired. Eden is now filled with the effects of rebellion—lies, loss of truth, breach of faith, alienation, and banishment.

The human story will unfold outside of Eden. The effects of sin cannot be continued in the Garden. They will follow the human condition. And the wages of sin is death.

THE CULTURE OF DEATH

It does not take long for death to become a major theme in human history. Motivated by anger and envy, "Cain rose up against his brother Abel, and killed him" (Gn 4:8). We see a lethal logic at work. The serpent is moved by envy to tempt Adam and Eve. Through their rebellious pride, sin and death enter the world.

More specifically, violent death enters the human family. The first murder is brother killing brother. From parents to children, what is learned is taught and passed on through the generations. Rebellion against God leads to violence and death in the killing of one's brother. Worse still, sin hardens the heart and removes any remorse for the taking of innocent life. Cain is not only a murderer but indifferent to the consequences: "Am I my brother's keeper?" (Gn 4:9).

God is not indifferent to the loss of life. Responsibility must be taken. Punishment must be rendered (Gn 4:11-12). The "crying blood" of Abel will be avenged. The very soil that soaked up Abel's blood will now turn against Cain. It will no longer yield an abundant crop. Cain moves further from Eden into the wilderness and finally to "the land of Nod," a place of desolation and separation from God (Gn 4:16). Disobedience has not yielded God-like powers. The Garden of Eden is but a distant memory. The land of Nod is now "home" to this wanderer.

THE MARK OF CAIN

Violence begets violence. Death brings forth more death. Cain, the killer of his brother, is now vulnerable to being killed. The taboo once broken makes it easier to violate. Once again, we see that a prohibition violated does not extend freedom but grows the virus of violence. But Yahweh is the God of life. God must act to curb the destruction. The violence of Cain must be met with the peace of God. The murder of Abel must not spill over to the killing of Cain. God's justice joins with mercy so that the killing will cease. Hence, God places "a mark on Cain, lest any who come upon him should kill him" (Gn 4:15). The mark of Cain is placed on him by God *for his protection*. Others may wish to kill Cain out a sense of duty, vengeance, or anger. But God will not allow the killing to continue: "If anyone kills Cain, Cain shall be avenged sevenfold" (Gn 4:15). The killing of Cain would not bring Abel back to life.

We see the risk of freedom and how its misuse can have deadly consequences. God does not cancel our freedom and turn us into robots. For the answer does not lie in a humanity without freedom. Such is *not* a humanity at all. Rather, freedom must be directed towards its proper exercise under the guidance of *truth*. God does not lash out in a vengeful way. God is the patient, loving Father who disciplines with justice and mercy. In the face of indifference, God cares. In response to envy, God encourages. In the face of death, God affirms the need to respect life. Even though Cain kills his brother, Cain does not lose his dignity as one made in the divine image. It is God who stops the violence, vengeance, and death by affirming life and personal dignity.

The culture of death and indifference is with us today. The lack of respect for life from the moment of conception to the hour of death is part of the contemporary social fabric. There is a coarseness and indifference that makes us numb to the needs of one another. We do not see ourselves as brother and sister in one family. We offer no response to the question, "Who is my neighbor?" (Lk 10:25-37).

The blood of Abel *continues* to find its way into the soil. The spilled blood of today cries out to the God who hears and cares. Do *we* not hear it? Is death too much with *us*? Are *we* not brother and sister to one another?

PRAYER

O Lord, you are the giver of life. All that is
comes from you. You create out of love and
your goodness sustains our life as gift.

Often, Lord, we turn your gift of life into a
selfish possession. We come to believe
that we live and die as our own masters.
We forget that everything comes from you.

When we see life as a possession, we begin to
compare ourselves to others. We are filled
with envy. We feel superior. With
envy and pride, we lose sight of you.
Others become our competition. We must
defeat them. Even violence and death can
be used in order to emerge victorious.

Lord, the culture of death is strong. Life is
at risk, especially for the weak and
voiceless. Help us to stand in solidarity with
the powerless. Let us lift our voices on
behalf of those who have no one to plead their cause.
In so doing, we follow your command.

O God, help us each day to advance the civilization
of life and love. Use us to be witnesses
on behalf of life. Especially give us the courage
and generous spirit to challenge the strong and love the weak.

Reflection Questions

1. In what ways have you experienced life as a gift from God?
   In what ways have you experienced the cross? How have
   your sufferings enriched your life?
2. In what ways do you struggle with anger? Envy? Why do
   these emotions rage within you? Are there specific individuals or circumstances which tempt you to hatred?
3. In what specific ways have you helped build the civilization of life and love? What kinds of opposition have you
   experienced? How has God's grace helped you to be courageous in confronting the culture of death?

After The Rain Comes The Rainbow

A popular song contains the following line, "Regrets, I've had a few, but then again too few to mention...." The song is entitled *My Way*. While the regrets may be few, sometimes our regrets are mighty big. We usually find ourselves lamenting, "If only...." Such is understandable when experienced by us poor humans. However, could we ever imagine God in a similar state of mind?

Maybe, we couldn't but the Scripture writers knew no such limitation. Yes, Yahweh could come to regret, even second guess, the decision to create the heavens and the earth. Well, at least Yahweh has been given pause to rethink the creation of human beings, especially creating them with freedom. Things have not turned out as expected. Somehow, freedom has become separated from truth. Freedom is reduced to doing as one pleases. *My Way* is no longer God's way. It is now the way of each individual doing his or her own thing. The result has not been a birth of freedom, but a fall into the bondage of sin. And sin is on the march. The isolated rebellion in Eden and the murder of Abel have now become widespread. Things are out of control, going from bad to worse. The writer of Genesis does not try to "spin" what is happening in God's favor. The somber reality is this: "When the Lord saw how great was man's wickedness on earth, and how no desire that his heart conceived was ever anything but evil, he regretted that he had made man on the earth, and his heart was grieved" (Gn 6:5-6).

The Perfect Storm

We are presented with a poignant picture of Yahweh as filled with regret at having created human beings. And so intense is God's regret that his heart is filled with grief. A question: What is God to do?

Regret gives way to anger. Grief becomes that righteous vengeance which belongs to God alone. Yahweh's soliloquy: "I will wipe out from the earth the men whom I have created, and not only the men, but also the beasts and the creeping things and the birds of the air, for I am sorry that I made them" (Gn 6:7). Sin was not confined to Eden. Yahweh's anger will not be limited to human beings. All of creation will be done away with. Perhaps Yahweh's anger is not just for his wicked children. Maybe Yahweh is also angry with himself? Why couldn't he have been satisfied with a nice garden and a bunch of animals? Why go and fool around with human beings? And above all, why give them freedom? No doubt the serpent knew what was going to happen. Well, there is only one thing to do—cut your losses and move on. Yahweh tried and it just didn't work out. Send the deadly waters and bring everything to an end.

The Ark and the Rainbow

Just as the waters of divine retribution are about to flow, we read: "But Noah found favor with the Lord" (Gn 6:8). Hold everything! God's creation will not be a total washout. Finally, there is one who is "a good man and blameless… for he walked with God…" (Gn 6:9-10). The anger of Yahweh begins to abate. Destruction will not be indiscriminate. God's righteous anger will be balanced by abundant mercy. Proportion enters so a saved remnant will abide. Creation will not suffer total destruction. Those inside the ark will form the basis for starting life anew.

After the waters "wipe out every living thing on the earth," Yahweh will establish his covenant of life with Noah. God's anger will never again reach the point of total destruction. God is the God of life. Time before the fall, now just a memory, is about to be reviewed. Creation is about to "take two"; this time with Noah and his sons. Noah is to multiply and take possession of creation. God is too committed to the work of his hands. God will not abandon humanity no matter how wicked. God has decided to stay the course and do everything possible to overcome sin. Even in the midst of massive wickedness, God will not turn to mass destruction. The destructive waters of the flood will recede and in its place is the rainbow. After the rain there is life; dark clouds give way to the multicolored rainbow of life (Gn 8 and 9).

There is much in our time which ignites the anger of God. Lent is the acceptable time to confront our sinfulness and face our wickedness. Our motivation is not to escape the dark clouds and destructive waters; but to be part of the rainbow of life. God desires our conversion so that we might live. We need not build an ark against the raging waters. We can dare acknowledge our sinfulness which is ever before us. For we are called to experience a deeper knowledge of God's mercy which washes and makes us "whiter than snow" (Ps 51).

After the rain, comes the rainbow.

PRAYER

O Lord, too often we reveal how much we are the
children of our first parents. We doubt your
word and we fail to trust in your promise. We
seek security rather than risk walking
by faith. We grasp the flashy and forbidden
rather than holding fast to your law.

O Lord, we too help to increase wickedness by
our own sinfulness. We are indifferent
to the needs of others. We seek our own advantage

and never hear the cries of the poor.
We contribute to the culture of death. We
work against the civilization of life and love.

Your anger rightfully flares. We no longer
deserve to be in your presence. We have
no right to hope in your mercy. For justice
demands our condemnation. But such is
not your way. Your steadfast love is greater
than our selfish love. Your mercy runs
deeper than the just judgment we deserve.

O Lord, give us the grace to face our iniquity
and acknowledge our sinfulness. For it is only
with such truth that we are set free to live
a life in your honor.
Even as the storms of our wickedness gather,
let us be ever mindful of your rainbow of life.

Reflection Questions

1. In what ways have you contributed to a general climate of rebellion against God? What effects has this rebellion had on others? On yourself?
2. In what ways have you experienced the abundant mercy of God? Does the Sacrament of Reconciliation offer significant encounters with the healing grace of Jesus? What obstacles keep you from confession? How do you intend to overcome these?
3. How have you helped others to experience the mercy of God? Do you find it difficult to witness to others about God's healing love? Why? What experiences have you shared with others? Have the experiences of others helped you? Which ones? Why?

The Covenant

Rainbows fade. Storm clouds reform. The destruction of the flood fades into memory and human wickedness resumes. Yahweh's struggle with rebellious humanity has only just begun. This time, however, God has pledged to forego massive destruction and struggle with the descendants of Noah. No doubt God must have wondered just what he was thinking of when he started all this. Especially, Yahweh must have doubted his own wisdom when he breathed that first breath into the clay figure. Well, one thing is sure. Yahweh's life has never been the same!

In place of divine wrath, God has decided to employ a different approach. Namely, God will enter into covenant relationships with those who live a righteous life. If God cannot have the whole loaf of creation to follow his ways, then Yahweh will settle for the occasional Noah-type in whom he finds favor. Such a compromise may seem shocking at first; but, on closer inspection, we see a glimpse of God's patient love. The original plan of paradise is taken off the drawing board by sin. Plan B—total destruction—was put on hold by Noah. Also such a plan is morally suspect since the good are punished with the wicked. Plan C—the covenant approach—will be in effect for the foreseeable future. To be sure the use of covenants will not be trouble free. In fact, a whole new set of problems will arise. But Yahweh is committed to the process as well as the substance of the relationship. The questionable aspect, as usual, is our vacillating response as fallen human beings.

A GREAT NATION

While Yahweh is not about to abandon the use of covenants to get his way, God is now upping the stakes and reaching beyond mere individuals. Yahweh will make a new covenant with an individual with an eye to the future. Through this individual Yahweh will form "a great nation" (Gn 12:1-2). Yahweh will once again create. This time there will be no illusions about perfection. Covenants call for realism and faithful love. Yahweh is more than up to the task. A new phase in God's relationship with his creation is about to commence. From humble beginnings God will form a people, a great nation, to do his will (Gn 12:2).

The Lord selects Abram. And unlike with Noah, there is no mention as to why Yahweh called Abram. There is a mystery about God's ways which are not open to full understanding. The call is a gift and the appropriate response is trust. Abram will certainly need a good measure of trust. For Abram must leave the land of all that is familiar and secure, and settle in a land that the Lord will provide (Gn 12:1). Beginning anew requires that Abram relinquish all that provided him with meaning, identity, and status within the community. Abram must become vulnerable and risk living securely with insecurity. Unlike Adam and Eve who sought security by grasping that which was beyond their reach, Abram must find security in receiving everything that the Lord will give. Our first parents covered their naked vulnerability. Abram becomes naked so that he can be covered by God's grace. The story of rebellion is now countered by the story of faithful trust.

With a simple eloquence that corresponds to the simple eloquence of Abram's faith-response, the Scriptures tell us, "Abram went as the Lord directed him..." (Gn 12:4). Not only does Yahweh provide a new land, but Abram and Sarai will give birth to a child, Isaac, with whom God's covenant will remain (Gn 17:21). A new phase of God's relationship with humanity is about to begin. From this initial call, response in faith, and miraculous birth, the long pilgrimage to Bethlehem and Golgotha is under way. The creation of Eden will not be destroyed; it will be redeemed. The initial covenant of creation will become in time the new covenant in the Messiah.

EVIDENCE OF THINGS NOT SEEN

It was just a short time ago that Yahweh was about to destroy all his creation. Along came Noah. The rainbow followed the flood. The covenant of life was established forever by the God of life. Yahweh refused to give up on humanity. His steadfast love endures and comes to one named Abram, who along with Sarai, will bring forth a son, Isaac. Through this child, a great nation will develop in history as God's people from whom will come the Messiah.

In all of these instances, there was ample evidence to despair. Yet beneath the surface grace was at work. In the words of the letter to the Hebrews, "Faith is the realization of what is hoped for and evidence of things not seen" (Heb 11:1). Lent is *our* time of faith in things not seen. No matter what our past, God offers a better future. Regardless of our sins, God's grace abounds the more. Even in the most lifeless of situations, God's renewing love is at work. Like Abram, God is calling us to go forth to a new place. The destination may not be clear, but the One who calls is worthy of our trust. God never fails!

PRAYER

O Lord, we find ourselves comfortable. We have spent
much time building our security.
The land is familiar. We are well off and well
respected. We don't want to move from
where we find ourselves. We know what we
have. We know who we are. Can't we
keep things on a simple basis?

O Lord, why do you keep calling us to go
forth? Why do you keep troubling
our comfort? Isn't faith in you about being
made comfortable when we are troubled?
Yet, you will not relent. You will not stop
urging us on to deeper levels of trust.
Why do you test us so? You know we are weak.

Yes, Lord, we know that in our weakness
your strength reaches perfection.
This is why we refuse to respond to your
call. We want to be strong in
ourselves, for ourselves, and by ourselves.
We want to boast of our powers.

Lord, help us to relent. Help us to give
up our pride. Let us in free obedience
venture into the land you provide. For
it is only with you, there is peace.
O Lord, be our peace. Even in things not
seen you are there. Strengthen our faith.

Reflection Questions

1. In what ways have you experienced God's call to grow in faith? How have you responded to God's call? What obstacles have kept you from responding with generosity?
2. What relationships have helped you grow in your faith? Have you experienced any relationships which have tested your faith? How have you responded to these challenges?
3. Has God used you to help others grow in their faith? How? In what ways were you able to help others overcome their fears?

Moses: Burden of Freedom

Freedom is a fragile thing. Easily abused, it is often confused with its dangerous imitation—license. As with most fragile things, freedom is precious and must be handled with care. Too often, the greatest of gifts are under-valued as we seek after over-rated worldly treasures. It seems we must lose, or come close to losing, that which really matters before its value becomes evident. A marriage and family can be taken for granted. A solid friendship can crumble through neglect. The same is true with freedom. We can easily lose it and hardly notice its disappearance. Our will can fall into bondage with ease. Freedom is not a once-and-for-all condition; it must be renewed each day.

As we have seen, there were times when God regretted creating humanity with the gift of freedom. The serpent exploited the gift by directing its use to an improper end. Almost from the beginning, we see that freedom separated from truth leads to tragedy. Freedom needs the guiding hand of God's truth in order to be authentic. License, freedom's imposter, rejects truth. The content of one's choices no longer matters. The only issue is whether one made a decision without external coercion. We fail to recognize that *internal* compulsion which comes from selfish desires. Truth is the fertile ground out of which freedom blooms.

There are times when *we* regret the gift of freedom. It would seem that life would be so much easier, less complicated, if freedom didn't exist. We could simply "do what comes naturally" rather than struggle against the tide of human nature. The gift of freedom can prove to be an awesome burden. At times we feel that we are condemned to freedom (Sartre). We want to escape from freedom (Fromm), for the burden of freedom is the corresponding weight of responsibility. If only we could have a freedom without being accountable. Such a longing extends deep into human history.

THE COMMUNITY MURMURED

The Hebrews suffered greatly under the lash of the Egyptians. Their slavery must come to an end. Yahweh hears their cries and *acts* to liberate his people. Under the leadership of Moses and Aaron, Pharaoh finally lets Yahweh's people go. The passage through the Red Sea into the Promised Land is anything but smooth. Israel is not on the "fast track" to prosperity and freedom. There will be a sojourn in the desert for forty years, a time of testing and formation. In the desert the Israelites will learn much about their God and about themselves.

We learn much about ourselves during times of adversity. Character, like gold, is tested in the fire. Israel will be tested in the barrenness of the desert. Unfortunately, Israel does not respond well to this time of adjustment from slavery to freedom, from being in an alien land to taking possession of the land the Lord will provide.

Israel *murmurs* against Moses and Aaron (Ex 16:2). Nothing directly mind you. No, the complaints are low volume and subtle, a low intensity complaint which dodges confrontation and lets the undermining of leadership continue. Life in the desert is not easy. You must learn to live without even some of the basics of life much less any luxuries. The Israelites even began longing for Egypt! Why? Simple. In Egypt there was, along with slavery, security. There was a structure which provided food and water. One may not grow fat or wealthy, but one wouldn't starve or die of thirst either. The security of slavery is looking better than the demands of freedom. This so-called gift of freedom is beginning to look like a death sentence to Israel (Ex 15:26).

FREEDOM'S SCHOOL

The passage from slavery to freedom is not easy. The desert serves as Israel's school. Israel must learn to trust completely in the Lord and follow his ways. Such trust and obedience is neither blind nor mindless. For it is only in trusting Yahweh that the desert will give way to the land of milk and honey. The desert, that place without distraction, confronts the people with their total dependency on God. Such a dependency does not cripple but fosters that freedom befitting the Lord's chosen people.

Lent is our time in the desert. The bell rings for us to come to freedom's school. Too often we try to ground security in the work of our hands. We labor against the day of tribulation. Such labor is in vain. It is only by placing ourselves in the secure love of God that we grow in freedom. But with this freedom comes responsibility. We feel the temptation to return to a former way of life. Better the devil we know than the devil we don't, so say the Irish. Yet this return to yesterday is not meant for God's people. We are a people of today and for tomorrow. We are a people of hope. And in the very desert of our everyday lives a flower blooms; a spring bubbles forth. Do you perceive them?

PRAYER

O Lord, your love for us is unbounded. Through
your gift of freedom, we are called to respond
to your self-disclosure.
You do not order us to love you. You invite us
to respond to your love. The risk of freedom
on your part is that we can, and do, say NO
to your invitation. The tragedy for us is
that we misuse our freedom in seeking only
ourselves.

You refuse to take back your gift of freedom.
You accept our rebellion as the risk of
love. Your justifiable anger flares. We have
caused you to regret, at times, the freedom
placed in our being. Yet you are overjoyed
when one of your children is found righteous.
The whole of heaven celebrates when one who
strays returns to your love.

O Lord, honesty requires that we acknowledge our
fear of freedom. It calls for us to be
responsible for our choices and the paths we walk.
With your gift of freedom, we must also
have your Paraclete of truth. Most especially,
we need truth. For without truth, we
fall into the chaos of our own desires.
But with your truth, our gift of freedom
is used to give you thanks and praise.

Reflection Questions

1. In what ways have you experienced the burden of freedom? How did you respond to the responsibility that goes with making decisions about your life? What guidelines do you use in exercising responsible freedom?
2. In what ways have you tried to avoid the burdens of freedom? What things seemed to offer you security? Were you able to reject this false security? How? Did others help you? How?
3. What spiritual resources have been helpful to you in exercising responsible freedom? In what specific ways has God called you to deeper levels of freedom? How have you responded?

Samuel: Speak Lord

Once Israel enters the land the Lord provided, a certain stability is achieved. To be sure there are external forces, hostile neighbors, which threaten Israel's existence. However, the Lord raises up leaders called judges who guide the nation through dangerous times. Israel is unique among the nations in that she has no king. Israel is the nation of Yahweh and he is the supreme Ruler. When Israel rebels against the law of the Lord, hostile forces arise to oppress Israel. When Israel repents, the Lord raises up judges to guide the people back into the way of peace (Jg 2:10-23). Again we see that Yahweh is much more measured in his response to Israel's rebellion against his rule. Gone is the talk of total destruction. The Lord allows Israel its freedom. When the people rebel, oppression follows. Yet the Lord is ever present to forgive and renew the covenant.

It was just a matter of time before Israel would want to be like the other nations. That is, Israel would want a king (1 S 8). Implicit in this request is Israel's rejection of Yahweh's rule. The Lord speaks through Samuel and clearly indicates the cost of having a king, namely, a loss of an entire way of life. The freedoms they now enjoy will be a thing of the past. The king will exercise absolute authority over property as well as the most personal relationships within the family. The rule of an earthly king will be much different than the rule of Yahweh. The people persist in their demands and so Yahweh relents. Israel will have its king, but with this warning: "…you will complain against the king whom you have chosen, but on that day the Lord will not answer you" (1 S 8:18).

Are leaders like Samuel born or made? Do leaders make the times or do events form leaders? Academics have debated these questions without end. However, from the perspective of the Bible the answer is clear. Leaders are raised up by God and often do not conform to human expectations. Those raised up by the Lord are entrusted with his message and empowered by his Spirit.

Samuel is the son of Elkanah and Hannah. His conception and birth is the will of God since Hannah was sterile. For her part, Hannah dedicates Samuel to do the work of the Lord (1 S 1:28). In time Samuel grows as a minister of the Lord during a time in which revelations were rare (1 S 3:1). Yet religious abuses are too much for Yahweh to endure. The house of Eli, which serves as the priests of Yahweh, has become corrupt. The priests are dressing properly and burning all the incense the temple can hold, but a pure heart is lacking. The sons of Eli were abusing the people and keeping the choicest offerings to the Lord for themselves (1 S 2:29). This must stop! Yahweh will send his prophet to demand reform or doom will follow.

Whom to send? In the midst of civic and religious corruption, there is Samuel who is young but "growing in stature and in worth in the estimation of the Lord and men" (1 S 2:26). In spite of his youth the Lord calls Samuel to confront the corruption of the priests and the shocking rejection of Yahweh by the people in favor of a king. Israel refuses to listen to Samuel, hence the nation suffers defeat at the hands of the Philistines (1 S 4:1). Things go from bad to worse. The ark of the Lord is captured and Eli's two sons are killed. The bad news causes Eli to fall and die from a broken neck. The situation is desperate: "Gone is the glory from Israel" (1 S 4:21-22).

God's people have established throughout a clear pattern of behavior, rejection of the covenant in favor of alien gods or some corrupt practice of their neighbors. The Lord warns them of impending disaster. The warning is ignored. Sure enough, Israel falls into bondage. Yahweh must act once again to liberate his people. A renewal of the covenant takes place. And so it goes once again. Samuel confronts the people with a simple option: "If you wish with your whole heart to return to the Lord, put away your foreign gods... devote yourselves to the Lord, and worship him alone" (1 S 7:3). Israel repents and returns to the Lord. The Philistines are defeated and Israel once again enjoys freedom (1 S 7:7-14). Unfortunately, the yearning for a king will not subside. Hence, Yahweh gives them a king, Saul to be specific (1 S 9:14-17). The subsequent history of Israel under Saul proves once again the need to be careful what you pray for; you might get it!

America has always understood itself as enjoying a special relationship with God. The Bible teaches that such a relationship is the call to greater responsibility in seeking justice, truth, fidelity to the moral law, and living with integrity. Repentance and renewal are not just for the individual heart but also for the collective soul of a nation. Lent is a fitting time to examine our national character and review our priorities as a people. We have been given much. Much will be expected of us. Those selected to lead must be men and women outstanding in virtue and moral example. We need religious and civic leaders who inspire us "to do the right and to love goodness, and to walk humbly with your God" (Mi 6:8).

PRAYER

O Lord, you are ruler of all the nations. The
peoples of great civilizations rise and fall

but you alone endure. You raise up nations
to do your will. Your power is felt
throughout the whole of creation and until
the end of time when you return in glory.

Time and again, the nations rise against you
and rebel against your holy rule.
The arrogance of power and the wealth of the
earth are used to affirm our goodness
and move us to prideful arrogance.

You, O Lord, scoff at such pretense. You
mock our claims to greatness.
You leave us to our own designs and
we falter. Without your law, we fall
into chaos. Without your grace, the
work of our hands does not endure.
Without your providence and love, we are
easily overcome and fall into despair.

O Lord, forgive our arrogance and form within
us a heart renewed. Let us be a great
people by seeking your will and letting
your justice be found in our land.
O Lord, let us be compassionate as you are compassionate.
In obeying you, we find lasting peace.

Reflection Questions

1. In what ways have we as a nation failed to follow God's
   moral law? What have the consequences been for our public life? How can we repent from such rebellion?
2. What role does moral character play in selecting leaders,
   religious and secular? What special challenges face leaders today? What are some of the urgent needs of our society? Of the Church? How might leaders respond?

3. What role does the community play in the formation of leaders? How does the community challenge its leaders to moral greatness? Do leaders reflect the state of the nation? The Church? How might leaders challenge the community to overcome its failures?

Ezekiel: A Watchman For Israel

One of the enduring treasures of the Christian spiritual tradition is the works of mercy, both corporal and spiritual. In recent times the corporal works have received a great deal of attention in connection with social justice: feeding the hungry, clothing the naked, caring for the sick, and a whole cluster of works for providing basic necessities to the poor.

Unfortunately, the spiritual works of mercy have not received as much attention. Yet, it should be kept in mind that *both* the corporal and spiritual go together in caring for the *whole* person. The spiritual works of mercy strike some as too pietistic, individualistic, and removed from the "real" needs of people today. The spiritual works of mercy may seem better suited to a simpler, less complex age. Their time has come and gone.

Nothing could be further from the truth. With a general renewed interest in spirituality, these works of mercy are essential for growth in the Spirit. One in particular is well suited to the season of Lent and to the prophetic ministry of Ezekiel. It is much misunderstood in today's "non-judgmental" environment. To be specific, the need to correct the sinner is one of the most important works of mercy one can offer to another, for the final disposition of one's soul often hangs in the balance.

However, the very notion of correcting the sinner carries with it all kinds of negative connotations: self-righteousness, arrogance, judgmentalism, and a kind of moralism that Jesus rejected. While admitting that these abuses are certainly possible, the task of correcting the sinner must always be done with *love*. The aim of such correction is to win over one's brother or sister to the Lord. Hence, the *manner* as well as the message is crucial in correcting the sinner. Also, one should always remember one's own sinfulness and weakness. We all fall short of God's glory. We are all in need of saving, amazing grace. At the same time, there can be no compromise when it comes to proclaiming God's word.

SWEET AS HONEY

Ezekiel is raised up by the Lord and sent to Israel in order to call the people away from sin. Israel's response to the correction is far from certain. What is quite certain is the word of the Lord made known through Ezekiel. The correction to Israel is put on a scroll and given to Ezekiel to eat. The word of the Lord must never be a mere external pronouncement. The prophet must internalize the word of God. The word must live in the marrow and intestines of the prophet. Ezekiel digests the scroll so that it may come out of him with authentic power (Ezk 3:1-4). The scroll is "sweet as honey" in Ezekiel's mouth. The Lord's word is bitter to those who refuse to speak the truth as well as to those who refuse to listen.

Ezekiel is not only a prophet but also "a watchman for the house of Israel" (Ezk 3:17-21). For Ezekiel must not only speak God's word, he is also called to instruct the wayward and ignorant. It is not enough to preach the word, the prophet must also provide a vision for living a life of fidelity to the Lord. Ezekiel is to be on the alert for all that may cause Israel to stumble by chasing after false gods. The Lord does not just hold the people responsible for their actions. The prophet will be held accountable if he refuses to speak God's word. Without God's word being proclaimed the wicked cannot turn from sin. They remain both ignorant and uncontrite. The Lord demands a great deal from his prophets.

Ezekiel is given a vision of dry bones by the Lord (Ezk 37:1-14). These bones represent the condition of Israel. The people have violated the covenant and find themselves in exile under the oppressive rule of the Babylonian king Nebuchadnezzar in 597. In 587, Nebuchadnezzar destroys the temple. The people refused to believe Ezekiel and now suffer the consequences.

Once again, the Lord refuses to give up on Israel. He gives Ezekiel a new message, a message of restoration and hope. Even in the midst of exile, the Lord offers a way home and a new covenant of salvation. The dry bones will have flesh grow over them and a living spirit will bring the skeleton to life. The Lord will return Israel to its homeland. Yahweh will once again be their God, and they shall be his people. The words of the Lord: "I will open your graves and have you raise from them, and bring you back to the land of Israel.... I open your graves and have you rise from them.... I put my spirit in you that you may live... you shall know I am the Lord" (Ezk 37:12-14).

These hopeful words of Yahweh will reach across the centuries. The graves of the dead will once again be open and the dead will come forth (Mt 27:51-53). At the moment of Jesus' death, there is an opening of the tombs to signal life's victory. On that first Easter, Jesus rises and forever changes the *meaning* of all tombs. For death will no longer have the final word. The dry bones of the dead will come to life at the Second Coming. We can live each day with hope in him who is our hope.

PRAYER

O Lord, your word is sweet as honey for all
who do your will. Help us to study
your word and let it become the
foundation of our lives. Let your
word guide our daily coming and going until
we come home to you.

Give us the courage to live your word in that
part of the world we find ourselves.
We feel the pressure to compromise your
word and do our will instead of
yours. We want human respect and to
be well thought of by others.
Let us, O Lord, seek only your will
knowing that in your love is all
we need.

O Lord, in our proclaiming your word, let
us not be arrogant or self-righteous.
As we call others to do your will, let
us lead with example. Make us aware
of our limitations and how much we fall
short of your glory. With such humility,
we can bring others to love you more dearly.

O Lord, at times we are like dry bones. We
go away from you and die from lack
of your spirit. Renew us. Give us your
spirit so that we might rise to new life.

Reflection Questions

1. In what areas of your life do you need to experience fraternal correction? How do you respond to loving correction? What was the last instance in which you were spiritually corrected? How did you respond?
2. Are you able to correct others with love? How do you know constructive from destructive correction? Is prayer an important dimension of fraternal correction? How does prayer play a part in your ministry of loving correction?
3. How do you resist the temptation to self-righteousness and judgmentalism when correcting others? Have you become more humble and understanding in dealing with others? How?

Isaiah: Servant Songs

If at the beginning of our journey toward the cross, it seemed out of place to begin in Bethlehem, ending the first phase of our pilgrimage with Isaiah seems out of character. For Isaiah surely belongs to Advent—Christmas and all that we associate with the birth of the Messiah. Clearly, the gospel writers draw heavily on the prophecy of Isaiah (Mt 1:22-23) to ground the birth of Jesus within Jewish expectations about the Messiah.

Without question Isaiah is a towering figure when it comes to the birth of the Messiah. The same is true when it comes to the death of the Messiah. The writings of Isaiah cover the *whole* of the salvific life of Jesus, his glorious birth as well as his death on the cross. In birth and in death, Isaiah is present. Hence, Isaiah is the most appropriate figure with whom to conclude this initial phase of our journey. We have contended from the beginning that the crib and the cross cannot be separated, but they must be understood in relation to one another. The figure of Isaiah serves as a splendid bridge connecting the Incarnation with the Paschal Mystery.

SERVANT SONGS

Within the profound and massive poetic prophecies of Isaiah, there are four gems which have been applied to the Messiah. Collectively, we term these four prophecies "the Servant Songs": Is 41:8, 42:1; 49:3; and 52:13-53:12. At times the Servant of the Lord is understood in a collective sense; that is, Israel is to be Yahweh's instrument for justice. The greatness of the Lord is seen in the way Israel is virtuous and seeks the ways of the Lord. Left to itself, Israel would flounder and fall into perpetual bondage. However, when Israel responds to the Lord, there is justice and peace. The other nations are inspired to follow Yahweh as well.

There are also instances when the Servant of Yahweh is an individual. The Servant of Yahweh goes to the people with the word of the Lord. The Servant of the Lord instructs the people in the ways of God and calls the people to conversion. As might be expected, there is often opposition—even violence and death. The Servant of Yahweh will also be called the *Suffering* Servant of Yahweh. The most moving passage is contained in chapter 52 (verse 13) and includes the whole of chapter 53. This particular song is especially rich in imagery of the Messiah.

SUFFERING SERVANT OF YAHWEH

In reading this beautiful song, it is easy to see how the Church associated it with Jesus. Jesus came to bring good news of peace to the Lord's people (Is 5:2-7). However, there is opposition by the mighty who feel threatened. God's servant is attacked and avoided by all the respectable people of the day (Is 52:14; 53:3). The Lord's servant is well versed with suffering. To the wonder of all, it is through this suffering that God's servant achieves healing and salvation (Is 53:3-6). The suffering experienced by God's servant is the result of the sins of the people. The Suffering Servant is innocent; yet he suffers. The Servant seems to lose everything; yet, "he shall divide the spoils with the mighty," and God "will give him his portion among the great" (Is 53:12).

As we read this moving song and apply it to Jesus, it is hard not to be troubled by the reality of innocent suffering. Why does God allow this to happen to his servant? To his Son? And yes, to us? This question is especially challenging in a culture and time which sees no value in suffering, much less innocent suffering.

What is redemptive about suffering? This question is as old as the Scriptures (Job) and as current as our experience with suffering. To be sure, there is a point at which suffering dehumanizes and turns one away from God. The only response (not an answer) given by the Bible is the figure of the Suffering Servant at Golgotha. The suffering of the world goes back into Eden with that first rebellion. Sin has wounded the very fabric of existence. No corner of creation is left untouched. From the forces of nature to the passions within the human heart, sin has disordered the work of God's hands.

The only redemptive response can be totally innocent love, taking on itself the totality of sin. For we are powerless to turn the tide of sin. By ourselves death has the final word. It is only with the gift of Jesus that the ultimate victory of grace is assured. It is a victory by tremendous love at a terrible cost—the crucifixion (Rm 5:6). With God there is no cheap grace and bargain basement love. The depth of sin's power to destroy can only be transformed by the One who is disfigured and then transfigured (Mt 17:1-8).

Into such a mystery, we are invited. All of our questions will not be answered. All of our doubts will not be dispelled. All of our fears will not suddenly vanish. What will be ours is a joy and peace that allows us to continue our journey to Jerusalem.

Prayer

O Lord, through our Baptism we are called to be
your people. We are empowered in the Spirit
to be your servants. We are to be a servant
for the Church and a servant in helping
to establish your justice and peace in the world.

In following Jesus, we bring glad tidings to
the poor, afflicted, and those in need.
We proclaim your greatness to all the earth.

We go forth to tell of your truth.
There is opposition. The forces of this world
do not acknowledge your greatness.
Violence. Death. Rejection. Help us to face
them with courage. Help us to know
that with you is redemption and life.

O Lord, in bringing your Gospel of Life we
experience suffering because of the
world's opposition. Let us not despair, give
in to vengeance, or become self-righteous.
In all that we face, let us trust
completely in you. You never fail us.
Your faithful love endures forever.

O Lord, let our sufferings be united with those
of Jesus. Let our sufferings be a source of
grace for others. Turn our cross into that
external symbol of unbounded love. Let us be
healed by the Cross of Christ.

Reflection Questions

1. In what ways have you recently experienced suffering? Have these sufferings strengthened or weakened your faith? What was the cause of your suffering—illness, accident, or sin? Were you able to share these with others?
2. In what ways have you been able to help others in their suffering? What special gifts has the Lord blessed you with in order to help others? How does prayer help you and others with suffering?
3. Do you experience doubts about God's love when you experience suffering? Do your sufferings help you to be more compassionate toward others? How? Can you think of a situation in which suffering helped you to draw closer to Jesus? If so, how did your relationship with Jesus become more intimate?

II

THE MESSAGE

In the world of politics, one of the cardinal rules is "stay on message." That is, find a theme that connects with the voters and let everything revolve around that theme. Above all, don't become distracted by side issues or controversies which may "turn off" the electorate. Keep your focus. Be like a laser-beam. Such are the essential steps for the successful candidate.

Jesus is no politician. Yes, he has a message. In fact, Jesus is *the* message he brings. Throughout his ministry there are temptations to tailor the message to fit the taste of the crowd. There are temptations to grasp political power and be the king of the crowd. There are even temptations by his inner circle to avoid controversy and skirt confrontations which might prove to be deadly. Jesus rejects all of these temptations. Success is not the primary goal of Jesus. Jesus is faithful to the work given him by the Father. The Gospel cannot be packaged so that the audience will find it appealing. Many turn away when they hear the cost of discipleship (Jn 6:60-71). Time and again Jesus refuses to become the king and usher in some new political regime (Jn 6:14-15). Jesus must even confront his own disciples with the hard truth that the Son of Man will be rejected, put to death, and rise on the third day (Mt 16:21-23). There is no attempt by Jesus to "spin" the message or curry the favor of the mighty. Jesus is the fulfillment of the prophecy of Isaiah: "How beautiful upon the mountains are the feet of him who brings glad tidings, announcing peace, bearing good news, announcing salvation…" (Is 52:7).

What is the good news announced by and embodied in the person of Jesus? The central theme of Jesus' preaching is this, "Repent, for the kingdom of heaven is at hand" (Mt 4:17). God is now doing a new thing. The time of deliverance and for decision-making is now! Each person must decide whether to continue to live in the same old way or to change and be part of God's kingdom. There is no middle ground. There is no legitimate delay in hoping for some more convenient hour. The kingdom, embodied in the person of Jesus, is *now* at hand.

Lent is that special time of grace to hear the message of Jesus. Let us be like that prudent merchant "searching for fine pearls. When he finds a pearl of great price, he goes and sells all that he has and buys it" (Mt 13:45-46). What we are seeking and being offered is a treasure beyond the value of the greatest pearl. Nothing we have can compare to the treasure of the kingdom. Let us seek and we shall find. Let us ask and it will be given to us. Let us knock and the door will be opened Above all, let us open ourselves to Jesus who knocks at the door of our hearts (Mt 7:7-8).

Jesus: Into the Desert

We are creatures of habit. Apparently, so is Satan. This is especially true when it comes to using temptations to rebel against God's rule. If temptation worked in Eden and with the Israelites in the desert who murmured against Moses and Aaron and fashioned a golden calf, why wouldn't temptation work once again? And this time the prize is even greater. The spoiling of Eden and the infidelity of the Israelites are nothing compared to the ultimate victory over God: getting Jesus, the Anointed One, to abandon the mission given him by the Father.

This time Satan will need to call on all his cunning if Jesus is to fall. No more forbidden fruit and golden calves. Jesus is beyond that. Satan must again be indirect but, nonetheless, make an offer that even the Messiah cannot refuse. One thing is clear from the beginning, namely, conditions favor Satan. Before the public ministry Jesus is led into the desert and "he ate nothing during those days, and when they were over he was hungry" (Lk 4:2). Yes, Jesus was led by the Holy Spirit, and Jesus is the Son of God; but, he is also human. The needs of the body are not canceled by the divine. Jesus *is* hungry! The devil is not far away.

TEMPTATION

The strategy employed by the devil is familiar. Jesus is experiencing a basic human need—hunger. To satisfy such a need is proper. However, the means for satisfying this need and what it reveals in the larger context cannot be overlooked. Jesus is not offered bread but stones. It is up to Jesus to turns stones into bread. In so doing, Jesus will reveal himself as the Son of God. Secondly, the mission of Jesus given by the Father will require a baptism of fire. There will be humiliation, suffering, and death. If only Jesus would worship the devil, all this could be avoided. All earthly power would be given to Jesus. Again, it is very human to want to avoid all this unpleasantness. It would be so easy to gain the end without the prescribed means. Finally, Jesus is brought to the top of the temple in Jerusalem. Who better to tempt God than Jesus? Just throw yourself from the temple and surely the Father will act to save the Son. What Father wouldn't?

With these three temptations, we see the master plan of Satan. The goal of the devil is to get Jesus to reveal his true identity *now*! Satan wants to reveal Jesus *before* the appropriate hour (Jn 12:20-26). If the stones become bread, the people will carry Jesus off and make him their king. If Jesus can be swayed by the love of power, then the victory of the power of love on Golgotha will not occur. And if Jesus can get the Father to save him from falling off the temple, how much more will he be inclined to let the cup of suffering in Gethsemane pass (Mt 26:36-39). The devil's one chance at ultimate victory is to keep Jesus from Jerusalem. (Down the road the devil will even use Simon Peter in trying to keep Jesus from Jerusalem.) It is not by accident that Jesus directs a harsh rebuke to Simon Peter, "Get behind me, Satan! You are an obstacle to me" (Mt 16:23).

The temptations of Jesus presented in the Gospel of Luke differ from Matthew's account in terms of the *order* of the temptations. For Matthew, the order is as follows: the temptation to turn stones into bread; the temptation to throw himself down from the pinnacle of the temple in Jerusalem; and, finally, the temptation to worship Satan in exchange for worldly power over all the nations visible from the top of a very high mountain (Mt 4:1-11). With Luke, the second and third temptations are reversed. This is done for a crucial theological reason. Namely, the climax of the temptations takes place in the Holy City on top of the temple. It is here that the ultimate victory of Jesus will take place. For now, Jesus will reject all of Satan's attempts to abandon his mission. This victory over Satan at the beginning of his public ministry is a glimpse of the final victory Jesus will achieve three years hence.

He Departed For A Time

Luke's account of the temptations ends on a sobering note: "When the devil had finished all his tempting, he departed from him for a time" (Lk 4:13). Satan will not give up. This victory by Jesus is but a momentary setback. Part of Satan's power is to get us to believe that watchfulness is not necessary. However, Satan is always on the alert to human weakness. In the words of First Peter, "Be sober and vigilant. Your opponent the devil is prowling around like a roaring lion looking for someone to devour" (1 P 5:8).

Lent is our own time in the desert. Daily we are tempted to renounce our baptismal identity as a child of God. Our temptations are less dramatic but no less real. In a culture which defines "being" in terms of "having," we are tempted to seek more than the daily bread given by Our Father. In a culture which loves power, we are tempted to seek our own ends rather than being of loving service to our neighbor. And in a culture of celebrity, we are tempted to public displays of ego rather than the quiet acts of love on behalf of others.

To share Jesus' victory, we must live by the word of God and daily make progress toward Jerusalem. At the same time, we must never be complacent. Satan departs only for a time. He waits another chance.

O Lord, each day we struggle to do your will.
We do not venture into the desert,
but we are drawn into the everyday realities
which make up our lives.
Your grace is present, but so is Satan with all
the temptations which try to keep us from
loving you and being neighbor to our neighbor.
The same Holy Spirit which led Jesus in
his time of testing must do the same if we
are to remain faithful.

O Lord, you offer us the Bread of Life, and too
often we seek that bread
which does not sustain us to eternal life.
We want power as the way of security. We do not
want to be weak and in need. We want
to provide for ourselves. Help us to grow in
humility so that we may receive from
you all we need. You are our security!

O Lord, we do not want to go to Jerusalem.
If you really cared for us, you would not
want us to drink from such a bitter cup,
or endure such a baptism of fire.
O Lord, this is Satan speaking. For it is
only by going to Jerusalem with Jesus
that we will come to know your saving
love. Let us not falter. Satan is near.
O Lord, be nearer still.

Reflection Questions

1. What specific sacrifices have you made during Lent? How
   have these helped you in your relationship with Jesus?

Which particular sacrifices do you find especially challenging? Why?

2. What are your most intense temptations? How does fasting and prayer provide you with spiritual strength? How have the Eucharist and Reconciliation been sources of grace in your life?

3. How do you respond to spiritual failure? Are you able to return to the Lord for forgiveness? In what specific ways has Satan been tempting you to turn from the Lord's ways? How have you faced these temptations?

As Was His Custom

Most of life is lived between the evenings. Sunrise and sunset serve as bookends for the lessons, good and bad, that are marked down for each of us. We delight in the moments of great exaltation and suffer in the shadow of the valley of death. In truth, however, the bulk of our allotted days is spent in ordinary time. For without the everyday, we would have no way of marking the peaks and valleys. Hence, even with all its routine, ordinariness and banality, the everyday is crucial as the stage on which the totality of our lives is played out.

Jesus has just completed one of the peak experiences of his time on earth; the temptations in the desert. This episode was filled with drama of the highest order, good contesting with evil. The stakes were high, the very ministry of Jesus. For the time being, Jesus has emerged victorious. The devil departs. Matthew tells us that "angels came and ministered to him" (Mt 4:11). Heaven celebrates this first victory! But there will be other contests. The time of testing has only begun. Satan will now turn his attention from this dramatic confrontation in the desert to the subtle texture of Jesus' everyday ministry.

THE LONG WAY HOME

Oscar Wilde once said that home is the place where, when you show up, they have to let you in. He might have added, but they don't have to like you. Jesus returns from the desert and starts to gain a reputation throughout Galilee. He taught in their synagogues and was praised by all (Lk 4:14-15). With the victory over

Satan behind him, along with a string of successful appearances in local synagogues, why not return home? Let the folks see that the local boy has grown into a man and is doing well by doing good.

Jesus arrives in his home town of Nazareth. He goes to the synagogue "according to his custom" (Lk 4:16). Even for Jesus, there is the need for custom. There is a ritual to our life which provides order and meaning. Again, everyday cannot be in the desert confronting Satan or traveling about to the adulation of others. Jesus returns home where he grew up, and goes to the local synagogue of his youth. He will do what he has been taught by his parents (Lk 2:51-52). But now, he will take an active role, that of an adult. Jesus reads from Isaiah:

> The Spirit of the Lord is upon me,
> because he has anointed me
> to bring glad tidings to the poor.
> He has sent me to proclaim liberty to captives
> and recovery of sight to the blind,
> to let the oppressed go free
> and to proclaim a year
> acceptable to the Lord. (Is 61:1-2)

Jesus does not merely read this jubilee passage from Isaiah, but he dares to indicate, "Today this scripture is fulfilled in your hearing" (Lk 4:21). Jesus is the Jubilee of God. With the birth of Jesus, the time of salvation has definitively broken into history. The time of captivity will give way to liberation. The effects of sin—bondage, blindness, and oppression—will be reversed through Jesus. Good news, sight, and total acceptance will be extended to all.

The reaction is at once swift yet conflicted. Luke tells us "all spoke highly of him" (Lk 4:22). At the same time they sought to remind Jesus of his place in the town. "Isn't this the son of Joseph?" (Lk 4:22). Translation: we cannot quibble with his message and manner so we will attack his background. This is the son of a carpenter. We are under no obligation to listen. Jesus lacks the necessary credentials.

Prophet Without Honor

Jesus will not go gently into that good night. He reminds them that God does not select his servants on the basis of human expectations. Elijah was sent to a poor widow. And the only one cleansed of leprosy by Elisha the prophet was Naaman the Syrian (Lk 4:25-27). In the beginning, the Israelites accepted Elijah and Elisha. However, in short order the people came to reject them. So it is with Jesus; the initial positive evaluation gives way to rejection. The townsfolk of Nazareth are so filled with hatred that they "rose up, drove him out of town, and led him to the brow of the hill on which their town had been built, to hurl him down headlong" (Lk 4:29). This rejection and attempt to kill Jesus is but a foretaste of what is to come. When Jesus arrives in Jerusalem three years hence, there will be the initial "Hosanna" that in one short week will be changed to, "Let him be crucified!" (Mt 21:9-11; Mt 27:22-23).

Satan did not waste time in resuming his attack on Jesus. Once again, the tactics change to fit the circumstances. The dramatic confrontation in the desert didn't work. This time Satan does his work in the marrow of Jesus' home town and uses a religious practice to which Jesus is accustomed. The familiar seedbeds of love will also sprout envy and violence.

Jesus came home but it was not to the reception he expected. On to Jerusalem! Shall we continue on with him?

Prayer

O Lord, we want to be accepted. We desire to be
well thought of by others. We crave human

respect. Too often, we are willing to seek
these at the cost of following your
holy will. We can't bear the thought that
those close to us will withdraw.
We too easily seek human praise
rather than your glory.

O Lord, help us to be strong. With the courage
of the Holy Spirit, let us do your will
and stand firm against the daily pressures
we experience to compromise your
truth. With the Holy Spirit, we shall not falter
or grow weak. We can inspire others
to follow the One who is Light and Life.

O Lord, sometimes our dearest friends and
loving family can be a cause of
our falling. Let us do the truth with
LOVE. In our faithful witness to
you, clean our hearts of arrogance and
pride. Let no self-righteousness
be part of our witnessing to others. For we
all fall short of your glory.

O Lord, give us the grace to follow Jesus
to the cross… and beyond. For in your
total acceptance, we will know lasting peace.

Reflection Questions

1. What recent experiences of rejection have you suffered?
   Why were you rejected? Did those who rejected you believe
   they were acting properly? Were you able to achieve reconciliation? Did the rejection turn out to be for the best?
2. How do you handle rejection? Do you experience the need
   to be accepted by everyone, even at the cost of some of your
   values? How do you resist those temptations?

3. Have you been able to help others deal with rejection? How? What was a recent incident in which you were rejected for following God's Commandments? Did you forgive those who hurt you? Did you become self-righteous? How does the example of Jesus being rejected inspire your commitment to the Gospel?

Give Them Something to Eat

A good deal of our success and failure in life depends on timing. From the serious business of comedy to the business of business, timing is crucial for success. The delivery of a comedy line and the delivery of a new product line calls for just the right moment. If your timing is off, the joke is flat and so are the sales of the latest "can't miss" product. Crucial to timing is knowing your audience or market. The comic and entrepreneur must be in touch with the taste of those who pay the bills.

Timing is crucial in the ministry of Jesus. His return home has been anything but successful. Matthew sums up the visit with the following pithy verse, "And he did not work many mighty deeds there because of their lack of faith" (Mt 13:58). Adding to Jesus' difficulties is the murderous hand of Herod. Word reaches Jesus that John the Baptist has been killed by Herod. Compounding the matter is Herod's belief that Jesus is John the Baptist raised from the dead (Mt 14:2). Clearly, it is time for Jesus to move on. The shadow of Jerusalem, with its legacy of rejecting and killing the prophets, grows longer with each passing day.

MANY NEEDS, FEW RESOURCES

While it was time for Jesus to move on, there will never come a time when Jesus tailors the message to the taste of the crowd. Unlike the false teachers of the day, "he taught them as one having authority, and not as their scribes" (Mt 7:28-29). It is because of the truth of Jesus' words that the crowds "followed him on foot from their towns" (Mt 14:13). The crowds follow Jesus from

Nazareth in order to hear his words and for the sick to be cured. The rejection at Nazareth gives way to the acceptance by the crowds who follow him "to a deserted place" (Mt 14:13).

Jesus, as the Jubilee of the Father, has before him the very ones spoken about in Isaiah, the poor, wretched, sick, neglected, imprisoned, and those rejected by the respectable folk. Jesus' response is beautifully captured in Matthew. "When he disembarked and saw the vast crowd, his heart was moved with pity for them, and he cured their sick" (Mt 14:14). However, the time has slipped away from morning into evening. A practical concern arises; one not lost on the disciples—it is late and the people are hungry (not to mention the grumbling stomachs of the Twelve). What to do?

Simple—send the crowd back home. Jesus rejects this impractical and uncaring solution by the disciples. Jesus shocks them by proposing a different approach. "Give them some food yourselves" (Mt 14:16). Their response is indicative of their approach to ministry and life. "Five loaves and two fish are all we have here" (Mt 14:17). The disciples are fixated on problems not ministry. They are keenly aware of all the obstacles to providing for the people, limited resources, overwhelming need, a deserted place, and a lack of money to even buy food. One thing is certain—the disciples are more in tune with the obstacles than with ministry. A sense of futility and passivity sets in. If something is to be done, a different response is required. Again, what to do?

Looking Up To Heaven

Practical needs must be kept in mind. Jesus is not unaware of the huge task before him. However, the paralysis that has set in has only served to make things worse. Jesus must act.

A simple action can have great consequences. Jesus has the resources brought to him and orders the crowd to be seated. This simple action turns the tide. Someone is doing something. The stage is set. Jesus takes the loaves and fish, "and looking up to heaven, he said the blessing, broke the loaves, and gave them to the disciples, who in turn gave them to the crowds" (Mt 14:19). This dramatic action by Jesus teaches the importance of giving thanks for what we have received. Once we recognize our resources and thank God for them, we can then be of service to others. Even if our resources are meager, when we give thanks (Eucharist), the resources we have increase to meet an abundance of needs. Without recognition and thanksgiving, our resources remain inadequate. The people go hungry. Jesus has the disciples distribute the blessed loaves and fish. After all have been satisfied, there is an abundance left over (Mt 14:20). The disciples have learned first hand what it means to give thanks and how gratitude can expand even the smallest of resources to meet the largest of needs. As in the time of Moses, as it is now with Jesus, God acts to feed his people in time of hunger (Ex 16:4).

So it is in our time. Jesus feeds us not fish and loaves, but the Living Bread come down from heaven (Jn 6:57-58). Jesus gives us his real presence so that we might rise on the last day (Jn 6:54-55). As we have been given, so we are to give to others. The needs of others remain great. On the natural level, our resources are small. Left to ourselves we can do nothing, but "with God all things are possible" (Mt 19:26). Every time a brother or sister comes to us in need, Jesus says to us, "Give them some food." As we look around at our resources, let us never fail to give thanks. In so doing, all will be satisfied along with an abundance left over for further service.

PRAYER

O Lord, we are aware of the many needs in our
world today. Poverty has not disappeared. The
poor remain with us. Many continue to suffer
a spiritual poverty, looking for that grace
which brings peace. Many are hungry for a
truth which does not perish with the passing

of time. We are hungry for the eternal in
the midst of the world's glory which passes away.

O Lord, we are equally aware of our many
limitations in serving others.
We find ourselves with meager resources
and the limited capacity to do good.
Help us, O Lord, to have our eyes opened and
our imaginations inspired to find
new ways of loving service. Help us to
be aware of all you give us, and to be
grateful for your gifts of every time and season.

O Lord, it is hard for us to be grateful. We are
at once self-absorbed and proud as well as
insecure and timid in responding to your
call to serve others. Inspire us to
know that with you all things are possible.

O Lord, let us both receive the Eucharist
and be a Eucharistic people. That is,
help us to be thankful for your gifts and
continue the loving example of Jesus.

Reflection Questions

1. What are some of the more urgent needs that we face in
   the world? In the Church? Have you been able to be of service to those in need? How? What kept you from using
   God's gifts to help others? How?
2. Which specific gifts has the Lord blessed you with in order to serve others? How have you given thanks to God
   for these gifts? How has the Lord used you in loving service in the Church? In society?
3. What are some of the major obstacles that have kept you
   from recognizing your gifts? What keeps you from being
   of service? What recent experience of service has helped
   you to see that in giving we receive?

Can You See Anything?

The philosopher Aristotle and the saintly Aquinas agree that our knowledge begins with the senses. The world comes to us, and we are connected to the world through sense data. Sense data is the raw materials out of which we understand reality. At one time or another, we have all asked the question: Which of the senses would we not want to lose? The loss of sight is high on the list. The Bible calls the eyes the windows to the soul.

The gift of sight has a spiritual significance. We do not see merely with our eyes but also with a discerning spirit. We need not only sight but *insight*, the ability to see with the eye of faith. We need to look beyond the surface to see the hand of God at work. A source of great disappointment to Jesus throughout his public ministry was the failure of the people to see the reign of God. This disappointment was most intense when it came to the disciples' failure to see the deeper meaning of Jesus' ministry.

A SECOND TIME

Jesus arrives at Bethsaida. His reputation for healing has preceded him. A blind man is brought to Jesus so the man's sight can be restored. Jesus withdraws from the madding crowd. Outside the town, Jesus places spittle on the man's eyes and asks, "Can you see anything?" (Mk 8:23). The surprising response from the man is: "I see people looking like trees walking around" (Mk 8:23-24). Jesus must try again. The second try proves to be the charm. Sight is restored and "he could see everything distinctly" (Mk 8:25).

This simple story teaches a profound lesson. The passage from blindness to sight, and finally to insight, does not happen all at once. There must be a growth in faith which brings things into focus. Above all, there is a gradual gaining of insight into the Person of Jesus. Even before Jesus' public ministry, Satan tempted Jesus to reveal himself before his time. A quick display of divine power and a spectacular declaration of Sonship is just what the devil ordered. The journey to Jerusalem would not be needed. Jesus could avoid the cross. He would also *avoid doing the will of the Father*. We would not be raised from the dead. We would still be in our sins (1 Cor 15:17). Jesus is showing us that if we wish to see him clearly, we must strengthen the eye of faith over a lifetime.

EYES AND NOT SEE

The story of the blind man at Bethsaida is a fitting way to end chapter 8 of Mark's Gospel. Throughout this chapter, we witness a continual inability of various groups, from the crowds to the disciples, to see the true identity and mission of Jesus. The irony is clear. The one born blind comes to see clearly on the natural level. Those who have seen mighty deeds by Jesus fail to gain insight into the Person of Jesus.

Chapter 8 of Mark's Gospel opens with the dramatic feeding of the four thousand (8:1-9). The response of the Pharisees is as predictable as it is tragic. "The Pharisees came forward to argue with him, seeking from him a sign from heaven to test him" (Mk 8:11). They will not accept Jesus but continually engage in disbelief. They will avoid seeing Jesus as the Son of God by attempting to engage in useless intellectual debate. The Pharisees continue the work of Satan by demanding a dramatic sign that will prove Jesus is the Son of God. All of this is useless as well, since they know of the healings and the dramatic feeding of the crowd, yet continue in their disbelief. No sign will help them see. Sadly, "...he left them, got into the boat again, and went off to the other shore" (Mk 8:13).

Once in the boat with his disciples, things are no better. Jesus warns the disciples "against the leaven of the Pharisees and the leaven of Herod" (Mk 8:15). This leaven is disbelief, lies, and murder. The disciples wrongly believe Jesus is speaking about material bread which they forgot to bring. Jesus is about to explode with frustration. "Are your hearts hardened too? Do you have eyes and not see, ears and not hear?" (Mk 8:18). Jesus reviews the two dramatic feedings of the crowds and concludes by asking the disciples, "Do you still not understand?" (Mk 8:21).

The answer is clearly NO! The disciples do not understand the bread, the teaching Jesus has been giving them. They have seen the miracles but still do not see the reign of God present in Jesus as divine Son. As with the blind man at Bethsaida, Jesus will have to continually work to help the disciples understand him and his mission.

The second half of Mark's Gospel (beginning with Peter's confession; 8:27) recounts the gradual process of the disciples coming to understand the bread, the teaching of Jesus. And what is this bread or teaching? "He began to teach them that the Son of Man must suffer greatly and be rejected by the elders, the chief priests, and the scribes, and be killed, and rise after three days. He said this openly" (Mk 8:31-32). The cross that is at the center of discipleship is the cross Jesus will first carry to show the way.

Peter takes Jesus aside and tries to tone down such talk. Just maybe Peter understood the "bread" of Jesus better than we thought.

PRAYER

O Lord, each day the wonders of your love
are made visible to us. We see your
goodness in the gift of life. We see your

might in the works of creation. We
feel your power with the rising of the
sun, and we are drawn into the
mystery of your divine being as we
gaze at the starry heavens.

Above all, O Lord, we see the wonder of your
saving grace in the gift of Jesus.
Out of your unbounded love for us, we
have been healed.
Out of your unbounded mercy, we have been
forgiven.
Out of your unbounded grace, we have the
hope of eternal life.

Yet, O Lord, our sight grows weak. We let
sin form a film on our eyes. We refuse
to look deep into the mystery of existence
and the gift of our lives. We are satisfied
to live on the surface. We are afraid to
go deeper, and look further into our
hearts. However, it is only in seeing you
clearly that we have hope of eternal life.
Lord, you ask: do we understand? Yes,
Help our lack of understanding.

Reflection Questions

1. In what ways have you experienced God's healing love?
   Were your prayers answered immediately? If not, how did
   you deal with God's delay in answering your prayers?
2. How would you describe your personal journey in faith
   toward Jesus? What have been the major crosses you were
   asked to carry? How did these crosses help you to draw
   closer to Jesus? Have you rejected the cross? Do you have
   any regrets?

3. What experiences help you to more closely see the presence of Jesus? Have you been able to help others see the presence of Jesus in their lives? How have you helped? How have the struggles of others been a source of inspiration for you?

A Canaanite Woman

The confrontation between Jesus and the Pharisees is nothing new. Their battle for control over the proper understanding of the law is intense to the point of death. One of the capital charges levied against Jesus is his serious disregard for the law. For his part, Jesus accuses the Pharisees of a legal rigorism which kills the spirit of the law. Jesus accuses the Pharisees of laying heavy religious obligations on the people but not following through with good example. The Pharisees, according to Jesus, pervert religion by seeking the external marks of honor and privilege but failing at the weightier measures of mercy and humility. Also the Pharisees and scribes perform all the external rituals of the law in order to gain the praise of others. But Jesus likens them to whitewashed tombs, "which appear beautiful on the outside, but inside are full of dead men's bones and every kind of filth" (Mt 23:27).

We should not get the impression that Jesus is opposed to the law. In fact, Matthew's Gospel goes to great length to show that Jesus did not come "to abolish but to fulfill" (Mt 5:17). It is Jesus' contention that the Pharisees and scribes are the ones who have abolished the law by substituting their own traditions and burdens as if given by Yahweh (Mt 5:20). The perfection of the law and prophets is not found in the tradition of the elders but in the words of Hosea, "For it is love that I desire, not sacrifice, and knowledge of God rather than holocausts" (Ho 6:6; Mt 12:7). The traditions and rituals are means of giving glory to God. The danger is raising them to ends in themselves. The golden calf is resurrected in a different form.

Instead of being constructed from jewelry, it is fashioned from our customs.

Regardless, it is an idol which does not give life.

ONLY TO THE HOUSE OF ISRAEL

Immediately following the latest confrontation between Jesus and the Pharisees over the law and human tradition (Mt 15:1-20), Jesus is confronted by a Canaanite woman with a need— her "daughter is tormented by a demon" (Mt 15:22). She wants Jesus to cure her.

The initial response of Jesus is shocking. "He did not say a word to her" (Mt 15:23). The disciples go even further. "Send her away, for she keeps calling after us" (Mt 15:23). The situation is starting to spin out of control, so Jesus must respond. And what a response! "I was sent only to the lost sheep of the house of Israel" (Mt 15:24). This response is even more shocking than the first response which was no response. Jesus is saying that his mission is restricted only to the people of Israel. This Canaanite woman and her daughter are outside the original mission given to Jesus. They are outside Jesus' zone of caring.

The woman doesn't know when to quit. She continues to press Jesus for a favorable response. Jesus' third response is even harsher than the last. "It is not right to take the food of the children and throw it to the dogs" (Mt 15:26). Jesus is actually calling this woman a dog! Can this be the Jesus of the crib; the one moved to pity by the needs of the crowd; and who fed the multitudes with meager resources? Is this the Jesus who confronts the Pharisees with their inability to show mercy? Jesus seems to be as rigid and lacking in compassion as any Pharisee or scribe.

The Canaanite woman will still not be put off. Her response to Jesus is nothing short of inspired. "Please, Lord, for even the dogs eat the scraps that fall from the table of their masters" (Mt 15:27).

Jesus knows when he's licked! After her last response what else is there to do but grant the request? "O woman, great is your faith! Let it be done for you as you wish" (Mt 15:28).

We must ask why Jesus acted this way. Jesus did not act Jesus-like. Several responses come to mind. Jesus goes through a process of growth in extending his message and mission to those beyond the house of Israel. The Canaanite woman may represent those outside the house of Israel who will come to accept Jesus while "his own people did not accept him" (Jn 1:11). Second, Jesus is giving his disciples an example of a narrow traditionalism which is lacking in mercy and compassion. Sometimes words are not enough. The example of Jesus refusing to help this woman in need may have been the shock therapy the disciples needed. Remember, they wanted to send her away. Third, Matthew could have used this story as an example for the early Church. The criteria for membership is not race, nationality, or status but a courageous, persistent faith. The Church is about inclusion and bringing to faith the whole world through the preaching of the Gospel (Mt 28:19-20).

The story of the Canaanite woman is a story of persistent faith. She had every reason to turn away. She did her best. Jesus had every reason not to grant her request. He came for the chosen people. What we see is the blending of two people who help each other grow. This woman's faith grows with each request. Jesus expands his ministry to those outside the original plan. In both, we see what a great faith joined to a great love can do.

Prayer

O Lord, we are well aware of our own needs.
Daily we lift our voices to you, knowing
that no prayer goes unanswered.
Yet, we often want immediate results. We

are not patient. We too often believe that your
delay is a denial of our need. We become
frustrated; we despair; and rely on our own
powers. We turn from you. We are lost.

O Lord, let us learn from the Canaanite woman.
We can always find excuses to give
up. We can rationalize our despair as *your*
lack of concern for us. But Lord, we know
we are fooling ourselves. We are avoiding the
challenge to grow into the spiritual life.
Too often we want your costly love, but we
are unwilling to accept the cross.

O Lord, we know that you always hear us.
Give us your Holy Spirit so that we
will persist in doing your will. In making
our needs known, let us be patient.
Let your Spirit quiet our inner tensions
and calm our restlessness.
We would like our faith to be great.
Truth demands that we acknowledge
our weak faith; limited ability to love; and
a hope always ready to despair.
Let your truth, O Lord, shine through our weakness.

Reflection Questions

1. What are some religious traditions that give meaning to
your life? How have these traditions helped you grow in
your relationship with Jesus? How have these traditions
helped you be a member of the Church?
2. Have any of your traditions become a source of difficulty
for your spiritual growth? How? In what ways are you able
to benefit from your traditions, but not have them become
an idol?

3. What part of your prayer life is devoted to petitions? Do you find yourself praying for others? Are you able to deal with God's "delay" in answering prayer? What happens if your petition is not answered the way you desire? Do you find it difficult to persist in prayer? Why?

What Is Your Name? Legion

There is no realm of existence that is left unaffected by sin. Nature is turned against humanity and will only yield its benefits after much work (Gn 3:17). Human nature is wounded and will ultimately succumb to the sting of death (Gn 3:19). Satan will continue his war against God and man throughout history (Gn 3:15). Sin has disordered the heart of the human person as well as the entire cosmos. The story of sin's pervasive influence can only be defeated by the ever greater presence of God's Kingdom. The central message of Jesus, "the Kingdom of God is at hand" (Mk 1:15), is not merely addressed to the individual but resonates throughout the creation. The message and Person of Jesus directly confronts the reign of Satan.

The most dramatic of all Jesus' exorcisms, that of the Gerasene demoniac (Mk 5:1-20), is part of the larger context of Jesus' ministry. The episode before, calming the sea (Mk 4:35-41), and the one which follows, the healings of Jarius' daughter and the woman with a hemorrhage (Mk 5:21-43), join with the exorcism to reveal the power of God's reign over nature; the healing of human frailty as a sign of God's ultimate victory over death; and the driving out of Satan. The consequences of the Fall in Eden are undergoing a dramatic reversal in the Person of Jesus.

DO NOT TORMENT ME!

All demons are not created equal. Some are more tenacious and evil than others. Further along in Mark's Gospel there is the exorcism of a boy by Jesus after the disciples were unable to free him from the demon (Mk 9:14-29). The disciples ask Jesus, "Why could we not drive it out?" (Mk 9:28). Jesus responds, "This kind can only come out through prayer" (Mk 9:29).

Returning to the Gerasene demoniac, his possession would certainly fall into that category. For this tortured man is not only possessed by an intense demon, but there is a tremendous number of evil spirits present. When Jesus ask, "What is your name?" the reply that is given is, "Legion is my name. There are many of us" (Mk 5:9). During this time a Roman legion of soldiers numbered 6,000. Also the evil spirits are sent into "a large herd of swine" (Mk 5:11). The herd numbered about two thousand. The point being, this man is possessed by many demons. It is Jesus alone who will be able to liberate him from his demonic possession.

The entire episode has a profound impact on everyone concerned. At the mere presence of Jesus, the evil spirits do him homage—"Jesus, Son of the Most High God"—and plead for mercy. The townsfolk are filled with fear and beg Jesus to go elsewhere (Mk 5:17). And of course, there is the demoniac himself who pleads to follow Jesus (Mk 5:18). Surprisingly Jesus refused his request and tells him to go home and proclaim the goodness of the Lord (Mk 5:18-20). Surprising because Jesus usually instructs those healed or released from a demon to keep silent. Jesus is always on guard against being turned into a political Messiah. However, in this case, the man will go among the Gentiles (the Decapolis) and proclaim God's mercy (Mk 5:19). The reaction of the people to the man's testimony is one of amazement (Mk 5:20). The mission of restoration and reconciliation by Jesus grows even more demanding and dramatic as Jerusalem draws closer. The work of Satan to prevent Jesus from entering the Holy City will only grow more intense and deadly.

The man who has been delivered from demonic possession wants to follow Jesus (Mk 5:18). A natural enough response. We can hardly imagine the sufferings this man has endured. Why wouldn't he want to follow the one who expelled Legion into the swine?

Jesus' response seems to be, well, surprising. Jesus tells the man, "Go home to your family and announce to them all that the Lord in his pity has done for you" (Mk 5:19). Why does Jesus react in such a way? The mere fact that Jesus healed this man does not mean he is called to follow Jesus in the same manner as the Twelve. It is Jesus who calls the individual. It is Jesus who initiates the invitation to follow him. It is the responsibility of the individual to respond to the call with the declaration of faith (Jn 15:16). Remember the rich young man. He wants to follow Jesus. He has kept all the commandments. There is one more step. "Go, sell what you have and give to the poor, and you will have treasure in heaven. Then come, follow me" (Mt 19:21). Unfortunately, the rich young man goes "away sad, for he has many possessions" (Mt 19:22). Jesus loved the young man, but he was simply *not yet* ready to accept Jesus' invitation to radical discipleship.

So it is with the former Gerasene demoniac. He is not called to a radical following of Jesus. However, he is to return home and witness to the reality of God's healing, liberating grace. In effect, there are many ways to follow Jesus. There are many gifts and vocations within the Church. The testimony of the man about Jesus evokes amazement from the people. In our own vocations, we are called to do the same.

PRAYER

O Lord, we are in need of your healing at every
level of our being. Our bodies are frail, and
they grow weak with the passage of time.
Daily we are reminded of our limitations
and the reality of death. This fills us with
fear; the dying of the light.

O Lord, we are in need of your healing.
Send your Holy Spirit to minister to our
all too human spirit. We easily abuse our
freedom and become slaves to our
passions. We refuse to grow in faith;
selecting security over the invitation
to follow you.

O Lord, it is only in your presence that our
demons of fear, despair, disillusionment,
and pride can be driven out. Too often,
we become comfortable living among the
tombs. All attempts by grace to free us
are met by our rejection.

O Lord, we know that you do not come to torment
us but liberate us from bondage.
Help us each day in the particular circumstances
of our lives to proclaim how much
you have done for us. Let us help others to
lift their voices in mighty praise.

Reflection Questions

1. In what ways, dramatic and small, has the Lord liberated
   you during spiritual warfare? Were you able to share these
   deliverances with others? How? What was their response?

2. How important is prayer in confronting those powers which try to keep you from loving Jesus? Do you employ formal prayer, or do you turn to spontaneous prayer? Do you find strength in both? How has the Eucharist been a source of spiritual nourishment for your relationship with Jesus?

3. How has the Lord called you to witness to his Kingdom within your vocation? How has the Lord's kindness been manifested in your life? Have you been able to help others experience God's healing grace? How?

Thursday of the Second Week of Lent
(Luke 19:1-10)

To Save What Was Lost

Time and again the ministry of Jesus takes on a human face. The incarnational principle, the need for the personal and the human, is uppermost with Jesus. Many of the debates with the Pharisees and scribes center around technical and abstract dimensions of the law. Yet Jesus always returns to the person and the power of the particular in order to reveal the reign of the Father. Jesus refuses to be drawn into debates which become mired in the slush of intellectual gamesmanship (Lk 10:29-37). It is this turn to the person that causes so much conflict with the Pharisees. Not only does Jesus respect each person, but in the estimation of the Pharisees, Jesus seeks out the *wrong* type of person. The Pharisees and scribes will charge Jesus with welcoming sinners and having table-fellowship with them (Lk 15:1-2).

A good example of the "wrong kind" of people Jesus attracts is Zacchaeus. His story appears only in the Gospel of Luke. To be sure there are many "reasons" to dislike this man. Yet for Jesus, there is one reason which trumps all the objections to Zacchaeus, namely, "...the Son of Man has come to seek and to save what was lost" (Lk 19:10). The mission of Jesus is not subject to human expectations, opinion polls, or even what some hold to be proper religious behavior. Jesus is the Jubilee and Compassion of the Father. Jesus comes to announce the time of grace. With Jesus there is liberation, release, and healing. If all of this is to be more than fine words, Jesus must take this occasion for table-fellowship with Zacchaeus.

A Bad Résumé

To say that Zacchaeus is unpopular in Jericho is a major understatement. One would be hard pressed to find someone more disliked. Just consider the following. He is not only a tax collector but the *chief* tax collector. Exacting tax monies for the hated Caesar will severely limit one's social life. Naturally Zacchaeus is a wealthy man. Again this does not engender good feelings, especially when Zacchaeus' wealth comes at the expense of his own people. Finally, Zacchaeus is short. Even then, there was a prejudice against the "vertically challenged"!

All of these liabilities could certainly be used to shun Zacchaeus and for Zacchaeus to give in to self-pity and vindictiveness. Such is not the way of Zacchaeus. He will get to meet Jesus in the old fashioned way—he'll earn it through persistence. Granted he's short, but that only means he'll have to try harder to be seen above the crowd. Hence, he climbs a sycamore tree. As Jesus passes by, Zacchaeus will shout out so the teacher, of whom he's heard so much, will take notice of him. But Zacchaeus doesn't get a chance to utter a word.

Come Down Quickly

Before Zacchaeus can utter a word, Jesus says, "Zacchaeus, come down quickly, for today I must stay at your house" (Lk 19:5). What an extraordinary thing for Jesus to do! It once again shows that it is Jesus who initiates the contact. It is Jesus who extends grace. There is no way to earn or merit what Jesus offers. The year of the Lord's favor is not open to human calculation or expectations. Grace is extended to all in need. The one addressed by Jesus is not asked for a list of achievements or a certificate of moral worthiness. Our deeds are straw and our moral worthiness easily becomes self-righteousness. Jesus' invitation to Zacchaeus is a splendid window into the very heart of God's way with sinners.

There is a sense of urgency and anticipation by Jesus. He tells Zacchaeus that he *"must"* have fellowship with him in his house, and it must be *today*. It is as if Jesus can't wait to welcome Zacchaeus back to the Father's house. Jesus is celebrating, like the whole of heaven, at the homecoming of this true son of Abraham (Lk 15:7; Lk 19:9). Joy is contagious. Zacchaeus comes "down quickly and received him with joy" (Lk 19:6).

THEY BEGAN TO GRUMBLE

There is one other obstacle that could serve to keep Zacchaeus from seeking Jesus and becoming bitter at the same time, namely, the judgment of others. When they hear Jesus will go to the house of Zacchaeus, they respond, "He has gone to stay at the house of a sinner" (Lk 19:7). This is just the kind of house Jesus *wants* to visit. For he came to seek out the lost. He came to announce the year of grace to those such as Zacchaeus. Notice that Zacchaeus tries to justify himself by ticking off all his works of repentance (Lk 19:8). More so, notice how Jesus does NOT even respond to this list of reparations. What is needed is grace. This is what Jesus embodies and brings in order "to seek and to save what was lost" (Lk 19:10).

Lent is that holy season of grace more than it is a time of justifying ourselves. We face many obstacles in trying to see Jesus. We may experience the negative evaluation of others. Our past reputation may be a stumbling block to our present and future relationship with Jesus. Remember Zacchaeus. Remember the Lord wants to, the Lord *must* stay with him. Jesus wants to stay with us. And he wants to stay today!

PRAYER

O Lord, there are many obstacles which keep
us from seeing you; that keep us from

accepting your invitation to fellowship;
that keep us bitter. We can always
find ways to avoid being present when
you pass our way.

Yet, Lord, it is you who seek us out. It is
you who desire to come to our
homes and be in fellowship. It is we who
need the courage to make you welcome.
We keep dwelling on our past. We know
our sins. We have allowed them to
turn us from your offer of grace and a new
way of life.
We must admit that we have become comfortable
with our demons and failures.

But, Lord, you will not allow us to be complacent.
Your joy is contagious. Your grace overflows.
In spite of ourselves we are drawn to you. We
must move the obstacles. We must open our
hearts to you and make you welcome. We too are
filled with joy.

O Lord, let us not be fearful or mindful of the
judgments of others. Only you know the
truth of our hearts. Only your judgments are
just. Only your word seeks and saves us.

Reflection Questions

1. In what ways has the Lord come to you during Lent? Did
you experience the joy of the Holy Spirit? How? Were you
able to share this joy with others?
2. Do you experience a sense of forgiveness and peace with
the Sacrament of Reconciliation? What are the major obstacles which keep you from confession? How do you over-

come these obstacles? Do you experience joy with the reception of Reconciliation and the Eucharist?

3. Have you experienced the harsh judgment of others concerning your spiritual life? How did you respond? Have you been critical of others? How do you intend to ask their forgiveness?

III

JOURNEY TO JERUSALEM

An essential feature of the modern world is the presence of great cities, London, Paris, Rome, New York, Tokyo, and the list goes on and on. These mega-cities are centers of communications, finance, culture, and all that we associate with modernity. These mega-cities also have their problems, crime, blight, overcrowding, and a general sprawl that is too often unfriendly to families. Yet with all these negatives, we are committed to cities and their revitalization. We still think that the city is the Mecca for making one's reputation and fortune.

Great cities are not the exclusive characteristic of modernity. The biblical world has its list of great cities in Egypt, Babylonia, Assyria, and of course Israel. And chief among the cities of Israel is Jerusalem. For Jerusalem is not just a great city and capital, it is the *holy* city of fulfillment concerning Israel's expectations (Lk 9:51). Even more, it is the city towards which Jesus' face is turned. It is in Jerusalem that the baptism of fire will commence, and the chalice given by the Father will be consumed.

The journey to Jerusalem is not simply about geography and the traversing of miles. The journey to Jerusalem is a spiritual pilgrimage which slowly reveals the identity of Jesus, manifests the Kingdom of God and the opposition of Satan, and strengthens Jesus for his death on the cross. Throughout his journey, at once geographical and spiritual, Jesus faces many obstacles. Some of the most serious deterrents are erected by his own (Mt 16:21-23). At some level, the disciples knew that to follow Jesus is to drink of the same cup and to share the same baptism (Jn 16:1-4).

So far in our Lenten journey with Jesus, we have heard the message of the Kingdom and the opposition it has aroused. As Jesus draws ever closer to Jerusalem, the forces intent on killing Jesus are gathering even now (Lk 11:53). Yet, what is Jesus to say? "Father save me from this hour?" (Jn 12:27). To do so would be to reject the mission given by the Father (Jn 12:27-28). No, it is on to Jerusalem with the same Spirit-filled resolution that led Jesus into the wilderness just before the public ministry (Lk 4:1).

Just beyond the horizon we are about to enter a new region, that of Caesarea Philippi. We are also about to enter a new and definitive phase in the mission of Jesus.

The Neighborhood

We are not only beings in time, but we must also deal with the reality of space or location. Both aspects, time and space, have a great deal of influence on our behavior and character. We can tell much about a person if we know when and where he was born. The more we are able to narrow the location of one's birth, the more we are able to understand some of the unique aspects of a person's character. Not only is all politics local, but so is the formation of one's identity.

Jesus is resolute in his journey to the holy city of Jerusalem. But along the way there are a number of important stops. We recall the episode at Nazareth, Jesus' home town, and his being rejected in the synagogue (Lk 4:16-30); the call of the disciples by Lake Gennesaret (Lk 5:1-11); the wedding feast at Cana when water became wine (Jn 2:1-12); the Samaritan town of Sychar and his encounter with the woman at the well (Jn 4:4-42); and the ministry at Capernaum where Jesus taught in depth about the Kingdom (Mk 9:33-37). In all of these places, and many others, a crucial step on the journey to Jerusalem is taken.

Of all the stops on the way to Jerusalem, one would be hard pressed to find one more crucial than Caesarea Philippi. Up until this point, the major theme of Jesus' preaching and ministry has been the Kingdom of God. The healings, exorcisms, and parables centered on the active reign of God in the midst of the people through the Person of Jesus (Mt 13:1-15). With Jesus' arrival in the neighborhood of Caesarea Philippi, a new phase commences. The reign of God is among the people in the Person of Jesus (Mt 11:4-6), but now we are going to have revealed the nature of

God's reign. That is, from the time of Caesarea Philippi onward, Jesus continually speaks of his impending rejection, suffering, death, and resurrection on the third day (Mt 16:21-23). The Kingdom of God cannot be separated from the Messiah as Suffering Servant. Jesus must go to Jerusalem, the place where he will give "his life as an offering for sin" (Is 53:10).

IDENTITY

To date, the disciples have witnessed the ministry of Jesus in making present the reign of God. In each region where Jesus ministered, there was considerable speculation about *who* Jesus might be. They knew he was more than the son of Joseph the carpenter. But how much more? The speculation has reached an intense level. Some think Jesus is John the Baptist; others believe he is one of the prophets (Mt 16:14). The association of Jesus with these greats indicates the esteem with which Jesus is held by the people. The association is also wrong. For there is someone greater among them.

Jesus does not allow the disciples to avoid the crucial issue of his true identity by repeating the standard answers. The question of Jesus' identity cannot be ignored. The answer given by the disciples must become their own: "But who do you say that I am?" (Mt 16:15). Simon Peter, speaking for the Twelve, responds, "You are the Messiah, the Son of the living God" (Mt 16:16). Grace builds on nature. The Twelve knew there was something extraordinary about Jesus. They knew God was with him in a unique way. They left everything to follow Jesus because they perceived, to some degree, that he had a special relationship with Yahweh. However, they did not know the full extent of the relationship, the depth of Jesus' uniqueness. What was lacking in their recognition of Jesus was completed by revelation. "Blessed are you, Simon son of Jonah. For flesh and blood has not revealed this to you, but my heavenly Father" (Mt 16:17).

It is with the sending of the Holy Spirit at Pentecost that the disciples will come to understand Jesus as the divine Son of God (Ac 2:1-41). For now, Simon Peter, through revelation, acknowledges Jesus as the Messiah. The meaning of this revelation will become clearer as Jesus draws closer to Jerusalem. It will also become clear that the disciples do not yet understand just what it means to say, "Jesus is the Messiah, the Son of the living God."

MY CHURCH

The revelation of Jesus as the Messiah is not confined to the Twelve at Caesarea Philippi. Out of this dramatic revelation will come the Church, the community of faith, entrusted with the story of Jesus. The foundation of the Church is the story of Jesus as Messiah, entrusted to Peter as the one who receives the keys to the Kingdom (Mt 16:19). The authority of Peter is a derived authority, that is, an authority which comes from Jesus. Those in authority who come after Peter receive the authority of Jesus and the keys as well. Hence, it is of the greatest importance that the Church of Jesus Christ always remain in the truth of Jesus as Messiah, Son of the living God.

The Church is entrusted with the dangerous memory of Jesus as Messiah. Just how dangerous this memory is will become evident in a few moments. Jesus for the first time will teach the disciples what it means to be the Messiah. It is a teaching which is not easily learned and often forgotten. Even with the gift of revelation and the guidance of the Spirit, the gates of hell continue a relentless attack. And while God's Kingdom will triumph, Satan continues the struggle by trying to keep Jesus from Jerusalem. Who better to lend a hand than the very one entrusted with the keys?!

O Lord, we have traveled with you and seen the
mighty works of your hand. You have healed the
sick, fed the multitudes, and driven out evil spirits.
You have taught in the synagogues about the
mysteries of the Good News. You have dared to eat
with sinners and teach parables to the poor.
You have revealed the mysteries of the Kingdom to
little ones, while allowing them to remain
an obstacle to the learned, the clever, and the arrogant.

O Lord, in all of these manifestations of the
Kingdom, we have avoided the question:
Who is Jesus? We are afraid to ponder the
answer and consider its consequences.
We want to be part of your ministry. We like
being given the keys and all the authority.
We like thinking of our Church as a rock.

What troubles us is the revelation that you, O Lord,
are the Messiah of the living God. We know
that this will require you to go to Jerusalem.
You will have to confront those in opposition
to the reign of God.
If we have been with you in your ministry, we
must be with you in your mission. And your
mission cannot bypass Jerusalem.

O Lord, we are fearful because our mission calls
for us to be with you.
Strengthen us for the journey.

Reflection Questions

1. How has your understanding of Jesus changed over the years? What are the significant reasons for the changes? What effects have these changes had on your spiritual life?
2. How would you answer Jesus' question, "Who do people say that I am?" How has your answer affected your growth in the spiritual life? What do you think are the major misunderstandings about Jesus in today's world? Church?
3. Do you believe the Church exercises its authority in the proper manner? Why? Why not? What are some of the reforms that we need in the Church for the 21st century? How have you experienced the Church's authority—as a service? As a form of power? How do you believe the authority of the Church should be exercised in following the example of Jesus?

Out Of My Sight You Satan

Talk about your impending reversal of fortune, consider the situation of Simon Peter. He received a revelation from God as to the true identity of Jesus as the Messiah. In light of this revelation, Jesus gives Simon a new name, Peter, along with the keys of authority to the Kingdom of heaven (Mt 16:18-19). Simon Peter has gone from ex-fisherman to the foundation upon which Jesus will build his Church. This is an extreme version of upward mobility!

Such a rapid ascent is bound to give anyone an acute case of vertigo. Simon Peter is still intoxicated with his new-found authority. The very Church of the Messiah has been entrusted to Peter. No doubt images of power and privilege are dancing in his imagination. After all, this is the Messiah who healed the sick, fed the crowds, and battled the religious and intellectually smug. This is the Messiah whom the crowds on several occasions wanted to make king. Peter will one day be in charge of what the Messiah leaves behind. For now, Peter will enjoy his new status… at least for a few more minutes.

To Jerusalem

The ministry and mission of Jesus now takes a new and ominous turn. It is a turn Peter does not expect. In truth, we do not expect it either. The costly grace of redemption and the costly grace of discipleship come into focus. For Jesus "must go to Jerusalem," and there is no turning back.

Lest there be any doubt about what is in store for Jesus and those who accept the invitation to follow him, he states clearly that he will "suffer greatly from the elders, the chief priests, and the scribes, and be killed and on the third day be raised" (Mt 16:21). And not only will Jesus suffer, but those who follow him will drink from the same cup and be baptized with the same baptism of fire. Jesus never deceives those whom he calls to discipleship. This is the complete opposite of Satan, the Father of Lies, who has deceived human beings from the beginning. Jesus clearly indicates that the cross is central to following him. The costly grace of the cross is the only hope of eternal life. The life of humble service, in imitation of Jesus, is the only path to glory. It is Satan who promises life through prideful grasping after that which is forbidden. It is Satan who promises that through disobedience one will grow up and be like God. In the end, it is the broken promises of Satan that result in banishment and death.

Peter seems to want to save Jesus from himself. All this talk of rejection, suffering, and death is not fitting for the Messiah of God. Likewise, all this talk of the cross puts a new slant on receiving the keys and being the rock upon whom Jesus will build his Church. Just maybe Peter is also trying to save himself?

Regardless of Peter's motivation, Jesus will have none of it. In fact, Jesus harshly rebukes Peter: "Get behind me, Satan! You are an obstacle to me. You are thinking not as God does, but as human beings do" (Mt 16:23). The Gospel does not record Peter's reaction. Perhaps that is as it should be. Even those with keys to the Kingdom are entitled to a measure of dignity! Suffice it to say, the rebuke served as a valuable corrective even to one who received a revelation from the Father. Grace does not eliminate the weakness of human nature. Satan continually tries to divert Jesus from going to Jerusalem and completing the mission given by the Father. At times Satan will even try to use those nearest to the Lord.

At the center of every temptation by Satan is self-promotion. From the forbidden fruit in Eden to jumping off the top of the temple in Jerusalem, Satan always tries to tempt by inflating the ego. Adam and Eve will be like God. Jesus will be the superstar. Hence, when Jesus lays out the conditions for discipleship, the primary requirement is self-denial (Mt 16:24). Without self-denial, there is no possibility of taking up one's cross and following Jesus. Without self-denial, the cross is seen *only* as death. If one stops being the center of one's own existence, then non-being will surely result. Satan continually banks on our fear of death and lack of trust to do his bidding. Satan constantly assures us that in placing ourselves at the center of things, we will find life. History teaches the tragedy of Satan's way.

Discipleship runs in the opposite direction. Jesus, in word and deed, indicates that in losing our life for his sake we find life. And it is life in abundance (Mt 16:25; Jn 6:35, 54). There is nothing we can offer in exchange for the life Jesus will give to those who follow him. Not the knowledge of good and evil, not the adulation of the crowd, not even the keys of the Kingdom can substitute for the gift of life that comes from Jesus.

The decision is ours. About this Jesus is clear. "The Son of Man will come… and then repay everyone according to his conduct" (Mt 16:27).

PRAYER

O Lord, we must admit that we are very
much like Simon Peter. We like the
signs of authority and power. We enjoy
receiving the keys and being the one
who is given a revelation. We also want
to keep Jesus from going to Jerusalem.
Yes, we know that at times we too speak
like Satan.

O Lord, we know what awaits you in
the holy city: rejection, suffering, and
the cross. This is hard for us to reconcile with
our expectations about the Messiah.
We want a Messiah who is victorious,
powerful, and will rule for endless
ages. But we know....

What is it Lord? You say we do have
such a Messiah? How? The cross?
Yes, O Lord, we know it is the
cross which defeats sin. It is
the love of Jesus which powerfully overcomes
the hatred of Satan. It is the Lordship
of Jesus as Suffering Servant that establishes
your endless reign.

Yes, Lord, we know it is the cross. Help
us to deny ourselves and follow you
into everlasting Life.

Reflection Questions

1. Are you able to understand Peter's reaction to Jesus' pre-
   diction about his Passion? Would you have the same reaction? Did you find Jesus' response to Peter too harsh? Why?
   Why not?
2. Why is it so difficult to practice self-denial? How have you
   been tempted to self-promotion? Have you been able to resist these temptations? How?
3. How have you practiced self-denial during this Lenten season? How has this helped you grow closer to Jesus? How
   have you been tempted to abandon your Lenten program
   of spirituality? How has prayer and the Eucharist been a
   source of strength?

Dazzling As The Sun

Selective listening is at once a blessing and a burden. It is a blessing for the good umpire and the best friend. A good umpire knows what *not* to hear. He is able to walk away and let the game continue without escalating the situation. He doesn't have what is insultingly termed "rabbit ears." The best friend knows how not to hear the angry word. She is able to hear the *meaning* of a statement and not just the words. Selective listening is a blessing for good games and better friendships.

Selective listening can also be a burden. Many friendships have been lost because someone (or both) failed to hear a crucial aspect of a discussion. The greatest plans can go astray because someone didn't hear a minor detail that turned out to derail the project. Failure to listen can lead to tragic consequences.

The entire episode in the neighborhood of Caesarea Philippi demands total listening if the whole of Jesus' message and mission is to be understood. Unfortunately, the disciples, especially Simon Peter, have been employing selective listening. They have failed to grasp the *whole* of what Jesus is confiding to them. The disciples, and especially Simon Peter, have selected that part of Jesus' teaching which involves the cross. And of course it does. But the disciples have been so preoccupied with the cross that they failed to hear the rest of the story. Namely, Jesus clearly indicates that on the third day he will rise from the dead (Mt 16:21). On that "minor" detail, the entire message and mission of Jesus rests. In the words of Saint Paul, "If there is no resurrection of the dead, then neither has Christ been raised. And if Christ has not been raised, then empty is our preaching; empty, too, your faith" (1 Cor 15:13-14). The cross without the resurrection breeds despair. The resurrection without the cross offers that cheap grace which does not save. The authentic following of Jesus requires we listen to the *whole* message.

A High Mountain

How is Jesus to break through the disciples' selective listening? More than words will be required. Once before, when delivering a great teaching, Jesus went up a mountain (Mt 5:1). Jesus, the New Moses, gave the crowds his extended teaching about the Kingdom and what is required for being a faithful member (Mt 5-7). Perhaps it will work again.

Jesus takes Peter, James, and John (the same three disciples he will take with him for prayer in Gethsemane as Jesus enters his passion, Mt 26:36-38) and ascends "a high mountain" (perhaps Tabor or Hermon). Once again, we see the connection between Jesus and Moses as well as Elijah. On Mount Sinai, Moses ascends to receive the stone tablets and is received into the glory of God. His face shines with the glory of God (Ex 24:12-18). Likewise, Elijah receives his call on the mountain of God (Sinai-Horeb). The Lord speaks to Elijah and sends him to do the work of one of his prophets (1 K 19:8-18).

In the presence of the three disciples (the testimony of three is accepted as truth in Jewish law), Jesus is transfigured (Mt 17:2). The connection with Sinai is evident. Jesus' face shines with the glory of God and his clothes are "white as light." But there is something and Someone greater than Moses and Elijah present. The voice from the cloud, the same voice which spoke at Sinai to Moses and Elijah, now testifies about Jesus. "This is my beloved Son, with whom I am well pleased; listen to him" (Mt 17:5). In addition to the voice of God, there is a vision of Jesus conversing with Moses and Elijah. This vision is profound as it indicates the place of Jesus in Israel's history. Namely, Jesus is the fulfillment of the law (Moses) and the prophets (Elijah). We are now to listen to Jesus, for he is the fullness of revelation (Mt 5:17-

20). Jesus is the One whom all the greats of Israel's past longed to see.

THREE BOOTHS

Peter once again assumes the role of leader. He offers to build three booths, one each for Jesus, Moses, and Elijah (Mt 17:4). The Israelites lived in booths during the sojourn from Egypt to the Promised Land (Lv 23:39-42). The Israelites also lived in booths during the feast of Tabernacles (thanksgiving for an abundant harvest, Jn 7:2). Perhaps, Peter wanted to capture the moment of glory against the harsh realities that lie ahead. It was not to be. After the voice from the cloud finishes, the disciples prostrate themselves. When they look up "they saw no one else but Jesus alone" (Mt 17:8).

The transfiguration cannot be captured in a booth or frozen in time. Jesus and the disciples cannot remain forever on a high mountain. They must eventually find their way to a hill outside Jerusalem. The disfiguration is not eliminated by the transfiguration. They form one reality in the life, ministry, and mission of Jesus, and that of the disciples. The ultimate transfiguration in glory will come on Golgotha (Jn 19:17-20; 28; 30) and the resurrection on the third day (Lk 24:1-9).

All of this lies in the future. For now, Jesus and the three disciples must come down the mountain.

PRAYER

O Lord, we must admit that all of the talk
about suffering, rejection, and death leaves
us fearful. We can only imagine what awaits
in Jerusalem. We know that if we accept
the call to follow you, the same cup and
baptism awaits us. We are not sure we are
up to the journey. We are weak. We fall.

O Lord, you are able to read our hearts. You
know our fear. As we go with you up
the high mountain, we are dazzled by the
vision and voice we see and hear.
Your being with Moses and Elijah fills
us with confidence.
Your being acknowledged as the Son of God fills
us with faith and hope.
O Lord, we want to stay on this mountain of glory.
We do not want to go any further.

O Lord, we know we must come down. We must go
to Jerusalem in order to be part of true glory
and eternal life.
If we want to see you transfigured, we
must also behold your disfigured face. The
glory of Mount Tabor is one with the glory of
Calvary. Lord, help us to listen to you.
For you are the Beloved Son of the Father.

Reflection Questions

1. In what ways have you witnessed the glory of the Lord in
   your daily life? How have these experiences changed you?
   How have they helped you draw closer to Jesus? To others?
2. In listening to Jesus as God's beloved Son, what are the
   major obstacles to hearing Jesus' words? How do you overcome these obstacles? Do you draw strength and discern-
   ment from the local church? How?
3. How do you deal with those times when Jesus seems to be
   silent in your life? What do you think accounts for such pe-
   riods? Are you able to continue your growth in the Holy
   Spirit? Do such times make you fearful? Why? What helps
   you during such times in your spiritual life?

Get Up! Do Not Be Afraid

Amidst the glory of the transfiguration, with its mighty vision and divine proclamation about Jesus, we are told the disciples "fell prostrate and were very much afraid" (Mt 17:6). Who wouldn't be afraid? On a human level, to be a witness to such a divine display would strike fear in any human being. Fear is at once natural and even prudent under the proper circumstances. This would seem to qualify.

There is also a profound theological reason for the appropriateness of fear. The Scriptures teach that the beginning of wisdom is the fear of the Lord (Pr 2:5-8), and one of the gifts of the spirit of the Lord (Is 11:2-3). The prophet Isaiah goes so far as to say the anointed Messiah's "delight shall be the fear of the Lord" (Is 11:3). Of course, the biblical understanding of fear is akin to awe rather than a feeling of danger or that which is unwanted. To be in the very presence of God is to become acutely aware of our inadequacy, impurity, and creaturely finitude. We are filled with the awesome majesty of God who creates all things by his word (Gn 1:3). We are at once attracted to and repelled by the One who *is* holiness itself (Is 6:3).

The fear which grips the disciples is at once humanly and biblically correct. Yet Jesus says to the disciples, "Get up! Do not be afraid" (Mt 17:7). Fear can paralyze. Fear can keep the disciples with their face in the ground. But even more troubling, the disciples may want to remain on the mountain of glory and never venture down to minister to the crowds. The temptation to remain on the mountain is even more pronounced for these three disciples. The talk of the cross has not been erased. The vision of Jesus' glory still burns bright in their minds. Why not remain with Moses and Elijah? Why not build three booths as a permanent shrine? Shouldn't the disciples stay on the mountain and listen for further revelations? Tempting questions. Much like Jesus faced in the desert. Satan never gives up.

DOWN FROM THE MOUNTAIN

Without a doubt, it is tempting to stay on the mountain. The tension is always present in the life of the Church, and the life of the Christian, between the glory on the mountain and the more mundane concerns of everyday life. Without maintaining this tension, we can find ourselves (and the Church) in one extreme or another. We can remain on the mountain, and our faith never touches the flat earth of everyday life. Our faith never becomes incarnational; that is, it never takes on flesh. A kind of spiritualism develops in which we avoid the call to love our neighbor in the concrete and the now (Mt 25:31-46; Lk 10:29).

The other extreme never looks to the mountain of God's glory, but is totally mired in human concerns. The need for grace to build on nature is never considered. Helping others becomes a total humanistic, social service which does not allow for the redemptive. There is a wall of separation between the natural and the supernatural. Yet Jesus has occasion to correct such one-sided ministry. To be of service to those in need is an essential aspect of the Gospel. However, the disciple must never forget that lasting joy comes because their "names are written in the book of life" (Lk 10:20).

The need to balance the material and the spiritual is powerfully captured in the Gospel of John with the multiplication of loaves (Jn 6:1-5) and the subsequent Bread of Life Discourse (Jn 6:22-71). The crowds have been following Jesus because of the signs he performed on the sick. In order to feed the large crowds, Jesus multiplied the loaves and fish. The crowds responded by wanting to "carry him off to make him king" (Jn 6:14-15). Jesus must withdraw to be by himself. He is not *that* kind of king. They failed to see the deeper meaning of being fed by Jesus.

The next day Jesus engages in a long discourse about the symbol of bread and the feeding of the crowds. Jesus did more than meet their physical needs, he performed a sign that would point to himself as the bread of life come down from heaven (Jn 6:48). Bread is the symbol of Jesus' teaching about the Father and also the sacramental bread for eternal life (Jn 6:54-55). Jesus responded to their need for food at the most basic level of physical hunger. Jesus built on that human need to show a higher need, a need for that food which is for life eternal (Jn 6:58).

Do Not Tell The Vision

The vision comes to a close. The cloud disappears. The voice grows silent. Jesus and the disciples must come down the mountain. Jesus instructs the disciples not to tell anyone about the vision (Mt 17:9). There will be a time to share what happened, when "the Son of Man has been raised from the dead" (Mt 17:9), but for now they are to remain silent. The talk of transfiguration, glory, and the voice of God will only make the path to Jerusalem more difficult.

Once off the mountain the familiar reemerges: Jesus heals a boy possessed by a demon (Mt 17:14); the disciples want to know why they couldn't drive out the Spirit (Mt 17:19-20); and there is a confrontation between Jesus' disciples and the temple officials over payment of the temple tax (Mt 17:24-27). And, oh yes, Jesus once again predicts his passion, death, and resurrection (Mt 17:22).

The response of the disciples? "And they were overwhelmed with grief" (Mt 17:23). Yes, the familiar certainly reemerged once off the mountain.

PRAYER

O Lord, we must admit our fears when it
comes to being with you.
We are afraid of what you offer. We want
to follow but on our own terms.
We are hesitant to go forward because
our past looks more secure. Yes, even a
past of sin and bondage can look more
inviting than a future with the cross.

O Lord, liberate us from fear. Let us be
filled with the wonders of your mighty
deeds. Let us see in Jesus your beloved
Son. Let us listen and follow him
from death to life. Mount Tabor is but
a foretaste of the glory without end.

O Lord, help us each day to tell the vision
of your glory. Not the glory of Tabor,
but the glory of your resurrection.
Let us live each day in the newness
of the Holy Spirit; the same Spirit which
raised you from the dead.

O Lord, we are not asking to be taken
out of our everyday lives. Help us
to see our everyday world with new eyes;
the eyes of the Spirit. Give us eyes of faith,
which allow us to see you in all things.

Reflection Questions

1. What are some of your major fears? What are the causes of
these fears? How do they affect your relationship with
God? With others? With yourself?

2. What experiences have made you aware of the mighty presence of God? Have you been open to receive the gift of the Holy Spirit—fear of the Lord? What mighty deeds of God fill you with a fear that attracts you to God? Those deeds which make you want to flee from God?

3. Are you able to find the presence of God in your everyday obligations? Are you able to join the physical and the spiritual dimensions of life in serving the Lord? How?

Within Sight Of The City

Jesus is finally on the outskirts of the holy city, Jerusalem. The journey has been long and grueling. Even before the public ministry, with the temptations in the desert, Satan has been determined to keep Jesus from Jerusalem. A decisive moment is reached, however, with the transfiguration (Lk 9:28-36) and Jesus speaking to Moses and Elijah about "his exodus that he was going to accomplish in Jerusalem" (Lk 9:31). Jesus is going to return to the Father, having completed all that he was assigned to do (Jn 14:30-31). The passage of Jesus from this world to the right hand of the Father will be accomplished by his passion, death, and resurrection. The new exodus accomplished by Jesus will be the passage from the bondage of sin and death, to the resurrection and new life.

After the transfiguration, Jesus "resolutely determined to journey to Jerusalem" (Lk 9:51). When Jesus emerged from the temptations in the desert, he returned to Nazareth and was rejected (Lk 4:16). Now after the transfiguration and his resolute determination to journey to Jerusalem, Jesus once again meets with rejection; this time by Samaritans who object to his going to Jerusalem (Samaritans worship on Mount Gerizim and not Mount Zion in Jerusalem, Dt 27:4; Jn 4:20-26). The rejection at Nazareth and this Samaritan town foretells the final rejection of Jesus at Jerusalem.

As Jesus nears Jerusalem, he offers a parable about ten gold coins (Lk 19:11-27). A king gives his servants ten gold coins to be used profitably. He returns and demands an account of their stewardship. Also, the king turns his wrath on those who rejected him as king. Jesus is telling the disciples it is crucial that they take all he taught them and use it for the Kingdom. Also, Jesus' rejection as king in Jerusalem will be overcome by his resurrection and ascension to the Father. Tragically, the holy city will be destroyed (Lk 23:27-31). But for now, Jesus is within sight of the city.

OPENING ACT

The journey to Jerusalem is about to be completed. There is a royal, kingly dimension about Jesus' entry into the holy city. As Jesus proceeds toward the city, "the whole multitude of his disciples" began to spread their cloaks and palm branches along the path (Mt 21:8; Mk 11:8; Lk 19:36; Jn 12:13). Jesus is the conquering king who raises great concern among the Pharisees. The reaction of the crowds causes the Pharisees to remark, "Look, the whole world has gone after him" (Jn 12:19). The Pharisees are saying more than they realize, for "the whole world" is called to be saved by the death and resurrection of Jesus. Salvation is not for the select few but for all who come to Jesus in spirit and truth (Jn 3:14-15).

The reaction of the disciples to Jesus' approaching Jerusalem is quite extraordinary. They echo the heavenly host at the time of the birth of Jesus: "Peace in heaven and glory in the highest" (Lk 2:14; 19:38). The disciples are "filled with joy for all the mighty deeds they had seen" and "they praise God aloud" (Lk 19:37). No doubt many in the crowd viewed Jesus as a political messiah who would drive out the hated Romans and reestablish the splendor of Israel under David. In order to correct this misunderstanding and moderate their excessive enthusiasm, Jesus mounts the colt of an ass. This symbolism calls to mind the kind of king promised by Zechariah: "Fear no more, O daughter Zion; see, your king comes, seated upon the colt of an ass" (Zc 9:9; Jn 12:15). And the promised king who mounts the colt is one who brings peace and salvation (also relevant is the prophet Zephaniah; especially 3:14-18). This is not the warrior king who brings about political liberation, but the king who defeats Satan and destroys the ultimate power of sin.

Rebuke Your Disciples

The reaction of the crowds as Jesus comes near the holy city is just what the religious and political leaders feared. Regardless of Jesus' words and symbolism, the crowds are seeing all this in political terms. The political authorities cannot accept any challenge to Caesar. The religious authorities do not want the Roman authorities to increase their oppression because of Jesus. The Pharisees and scribes have become comfortable with the status quo. The religious authorities want to protect their privilege and power.

As Jesus is moving along, the Pharisees demand that he put an end to this dangerous display. "Teacher, rebuke your disciples" (Lk 19:39). This is always the reaction of those whose power is threatened. Demand silence! Make the people go back to the way things used to be. All of this emotional display is dangerous. Jesus must stop troubling the comfortable and start bringing comfort to the authorities who are troubled.

Jesus' response is direct. "I tell you, if they keep silent, the stones will cry out!" (Lk 19:40). The Pharisees fail to see that there is more at work here than mere human enthusiasm. The Holy Spirit is at work. The coming of Jesus into the holy city marks a decisive moment in salvation history. The new covenant in the Spirit is about to commence. It is a time of joy, praise, and salvation. Even if the crowds would grow silent, the stones would give testimony to Jesus.

PRAYER

O Lord, we have followed you to the edge of the
holy city. Honesty requires that we acknowledge
our doubts, and even fear, about following you. We
know this is the city of your baptism of
fire. It will be ours as well.

But now, Lord, we are here with you. We
are about to enter Jerusalem. The crowds
are large and vocal. It is hard for us not
to be swept up in the moment. We
hear voices proclaiming you king. We
see the signs of respect and authority.
The palm branches and cloaks are placed
along your path. We can't help but
be impressed. We feel fortunate to be present.

Yet just as we began to feel comfortable, you
mount the colt of an ass. You are the king of
peace and salvation. The power you bring is
that of love. The victory you achieve over
sin comes by way of the cross. The Pharisees
are once again in opposition. Even in this
holy city, at this splendid moment, we cannot
get away from the cross.

O Lord, now that we have arrived at
Jerusalem, let's enjoy the moment. Just
for a little while, let us forget the cross.
What? If you keep quiet the stones would do what?

Reflection Questions

1. In what ways have you spiritually grown during your journey with Jesus to Jerusalem? What were the moments of
   greatest fear? What kept you following Jesus?

2. In what ways have you been tempted to be silent about the mighty deeds of God? How did you respond to such temptations? Have you been able to draw strength from the local church in witnessing to the mighty deeds of God? How?
3. Have you been able to help others realize the mighty deeds of God in their lives? How? Are others afraid of recognizing such works of God? Why? How have you grown in openness to the Holy Spirit's call to joy and praise of God?

IV

THE TIME OF VISITATION

First impressions and initial reactions can be quite misleading. The need for prudent evaluation often takes time. The outcome of an event, or the real character of a person, is seldom revealed with the initial episode. We must look for a pattern to emerge. We rush to judgment often to our sorrow.

Even before his public ministry, Jesus' destiny was inextricably tied to the holy city of Jerusalem. Throughout the public ministry, Satan continues to try and divert Jesus from Jerusalem and his destiny. Even the disciples, especially Simon Peter, try to spare Jesus from the fate that awaits. Jesus is equally determined to enter the holy city. And so he is within sight.

The initial reaction to Jesus by the crowds is overwhelming. It would seem that the geographical and spiritual journey was well worth the effort. Who would not be enlivened by crowds spreading their cloaks and palm branches on the ground in order to acknowledge the kingship of Jesus? Who would not be renewed at the words of the disciples as they praise God for all the mighty deeds performed through Jesus? And most satisfying of all, the Pharisees are besides themselves with envy. Throughout Jesus' travels and ministry, the religious leaders have rejected him. No personal or professional attack on Jesus was deemed out of bounds. Jesus was just the son of Joseph, a common workman. The Pharisees accused Jesus of being born out of wedlock, hence illegitimate (Jn 8:39-47). Worse still, the Pharisees accuse Jesus of being possessed by the devil (Jn 8:52). Yet now, just outside the holy city, Jesus is acclaimed by what the Pharisees deem to be "the whole world." "Hosanna! Blessed is he who comes in the name of the Lord, the king of Israel" (Jn 12:13). How satisfying for Jesus!

The initial report reaching the holy city is quite favorable to Jesus. The place is abuzz with rumor, report, and expectation of what might happen next. It is as if a high, human wave of excitement is about to descend upon Jerusalem. The holy city is about to be visited by her king. The Messiah of God approaches for the final act in establishing the Father's Kingdom. The time of visitation is at hand!

But wait. There is a commotion at the front of the procession. Things have come to a halt. Perhaps the Pharisees or even the Roman soldiers are preventing Jesus from entering the holy city. Jesus is so close, yet so far. Surely God will intervene to see that his beloved Son is heard in Jerusalem.

On closer inspection, there are no Pharisees or Roman troops blocking Jesus' entrance into the city. For some reason, Jesus has stopped on his own accord. At this moment, his gaze is transfixed on Jerusalem. The crowds grow silent as if in the presence of the divine. Jesus seems to be....

But why?

He Wept

Tears are nature's way of cleansing the eyes. On a deeper level, tears express emotions and purge the psyche. Tears can express a number of emotions—joy at winning the game; sorrow for a painful loss; relief at being released from a great pressure; shock at an unexpected outcome. Tears cover a wide range of emotions; and often more than one set of emotions at a time.

Some cultures are more at home with tears than others. Certain cultures view tears as a sign of weakness ("real men don't cry") or allow only women to cry. Other cultures are more expressive and view the shedding of tears as an appropriate way of responding to certain circumstances. In fact, it would seem strange *not* to cry. Within various ethnic groups, genders, and cultures the place of tears is quite complex and revelatory of our sophisticated emotional makeup.

As Jesus draws near to Jerusalem, Saint Luke tells us that Jesus "wept over it" (Lk 19:41). Perhaps there are tears of joy in response to the enthusiastic welcome Jesus received as he approached Jerusalem. Maybe Jesus was crying as a kind of emotional release. He had struggled so hard and waited so long to arrive at the holy city. Finally the goal is within sight. Jesus simply couldn't contain himself any longer. There are certainly plausible explanations. However, they are inaccurate. There is another reason why Jesus weeps at the sight of Jerusalem.

Jesus is able to view the city in its entirety from his vantage point on the Mount of Olives. The long unfolding of salvation history, from the initial promise of a savior in Eden until this very moment, should be a time of exaltation. The God who makes promises keeps them. The promise of the Messiah was not mere words, but the faithful love of Yahweh for his people. That love has become visible in Jesus. The year of the Lord's favor is about to enter Jerusalem. Yet Jesus is weeping over the city. Why?

Hidden From Your Eyes

The Gospels record two instances in which Jesus wept, the death of Lazarus (Jn 11:33), and over the holy city of Jerusalem. In both instances, Jesus' tears came from his deep sadness over the situation. Jesus loved Lazarus and his two sisters, Martha and Mary (Jn 11:5). The news of Lazarus' death evokes in Jesus a sadness which brings tears, a very human response at the death of a loved one.

Jesus weeps over Jerusalem; and, in many ways, it is over the approaching death of this holy city. Jerusalem does not recognize the time of its visitation. Jerusalem seeks to find peace through accommodation with the Romans, all the while plotting rebellion so as to reestablish the glory of David's rule. Even among the followers of Jesus, there is a persistent drive to turn Jesus into a political ruler. None of these hopes or strategies will work. The time of peace for Jerusalem waits just outside the city gates. The one who is peace comes on a colt with the good news of salvation that would be won through his death and resurrection. Nothing of what Jesus has to offer will be accepted. The rejection of Jesus at Nazareth, at the opening of the public ministry is completed with his resurrection in Jerusalem. The tears Jesus sheds are not for himself but for the holy city which will once again slay the prophet sent by Yahweh. And there is something greater than any prophet. Jerusalem will slay the Messiah! The opportunity for reconciliation and peace is now past. The peace Jesus offers is now "hidden from your eyes" (Lk 19:42). The tragedy of Jesus' entry into Jerusalem results from the people's failure "to recognize the time of [their] visitation" (Lk 19:44). The lament by Jesus over Jerusalem finds an echo in the Prologue to the Fourth Gospel: "He came to what was his own, but his own people did not accept him" (Jn 1:11).

THE DAYS ARE COMING

Jesus loves Jerusalem. Yet even divine love cannot overcome the refusal to accept the Messiah. The people are free to accept or reject Jesus. The fate of the city will be determined by their decision. The tears of Jesus indicate the destruction that will befall Jerusalem. "For the days are coming upon you when your enemies will raise a palisade against you; they will encircle you and hem you in on all sides. They will smash you to the ground and your children within you, and they will not leave one stone upon another within you…" (Lk 19:43-44). These events of destruction will take place in the future. The Romans will encircle the city and bring about its destruction (70 A.D.). No one should take comfort in the fall of Jerusalem. God's holy city will once again suffer the consequences of refusing that which brings peace—Jesus and the Gospel.

The destruction of Jerusalem lies in the future. Yet we see the decisions made in the present always have consequences beyond the current moment. The seeds of today yield the harvest of tomorrow. For now, however, the tears will dry. Jesus is going to enter the city for the final phase of his public ministry. He will teach in the temple area and engage in a final showdown with the Pharisees. Such a public display by Jesus cannot be tolerated. The forces of death are gathering at the very moment Jesus is about to perform the greatest of his signs (Lk 22:1-6; Jn 11:1-44).

O Lord, help us each day to know the
time of our visitation. For in being
open to you, we find the things that
are for our peace. With you alone
is salvation and the victory over sin
and death.

Yet Lord, we must admit that we are
so easily distracted. We try to
find peace in the things of this
world rather than in the world to come.
We chase after the false promises
of materialism. We find ourselves
empty and confused.

Lord, let us each day prepare for your
coming. For in truth you pass us
each day in our neighbor, in the goods
we enjoy, and, yes, in the crosses
we can unite with yours in the name
of redemptive love.

Lord, let us sing out your goodness with
our lives. Let us be ever mindful of
your mighty deeds. Above all, let us be
thankful for the many gifts of the Spirit
poured into our hearts daily. Blessed is
our Lord who comes to give us peace.

Reflection Questions

1. Have you been alert to the Lord's presence in your daily
   life? How? What have been the major obstacles which keep
   you from being attentive to Jesus? How do you intend to
   overcome these distractions?

2. What is your reaction to Jesus' weeping over Jerusalem? Have you had similar experiences of disappointment which moved you to tears? How did you respond to such disappointment? Did your relationship with Jesus become stronger? Weaker? Why?
3. What happens when nations turn away from God? What lessons can we learn from the destruction of Jerusalem by the Romans during the time of Jesus? Can we in America learn from the fall of Jerusalem? Can we learn from the fall of great nations throughout history? What does history teach us? Why do we fail to learn from the past?

Take Away The Stone

Jesus enters Jerusalem, and there is an immediate confrontation with those who are plotting his death (chief priests, scribes, and leaders, Lk 19:47) over the selling in the temple. Those in opposition want to kill Jesus right there, "but they could find no way to accomplish their purpose because all the people were hanging on his words" (Lk 19:48). As the days go by, the level of hostility increases. Jesus is continually questioned about his own authority as teacher, and he is questioned about various controversial issues from paying taxes to the coming of the Son of Man (Lk 20:1-8; 20:20-26; 21:20-28). By day Jesus teaches in the temple area. Large crowds come early and stay late in order to hear his words. However, it is too dangerous to stay in Jerusalem at night. Jesus must leave the city. He finds refuge "at the place called the Mount of Olives" (Lk 21:37). This will be the same place Jesus will withdraw to for prayer as he enters into his agony in the garden (Lk 22:39-46). For now it is a place of refuge.

The One You Love Is Ill

The plot to kill Jesus was not hatched in Jerusalem; it simply reaches its culmination in the holy city. Early on Jesus attracts the ire of the authorities (Lk 5:21). Jesus also attracts huge crowds which flames the passions of jealousy and envy in the Pharisees (Lk 6:17-19). However, there is a match which lights the fuse of the plan to kill Jesus. It is the supreme irony that what dooms Jesus to death is the greatest of his signs on behalf of life. Yet we have seen throughout, that the One who is the Resurrection and the Life must continually confront the forces of disbelief and death.

Word comes to Jesus that a dear friend, Lazarus, is ill (Jn 11:2). In a strange way, Jesus does not leave quickly for Bethany to be with Lazarus, Martha and Mary, whom Jesus loves (Jn 11:5). He waits a full two days before leaving. By the time he arrives at Bethany, Lazarus has been in the tomb four days (the length of time it was believed the soul separated from the body). Lazarus is not asleep, but dead (Jn 11:14). While Jesus is still at a distance from Bethany, Martha goes to meet Jesus. Her greeting to Jesus is at once restrained as well as direct: "Lord, if you had been here, my brother would not have died" (Jn 11:21). There is an edge to her words. If Jesus had come when first told of her brother's illness, Lazarus would still be alive.

Jesus' delay was not his denial of love for Lazarus, nor was it indifference to the concern of Martha. The illness and death of Lazarus is an occasion for the Father of Life to be revealed through Jesus (Jn 11:4). The rebuke by Martha about Jesus' delay is an opportunity for him to draw her into a proclamation of faith (Jn 11:27). God's grace continually shines through the seemingly lifeless; human weakness is made strong by Jesus' strengthening a weak faith.

The Gospel of John contains seven signs (2:1-11; 4:46-54; 5:1-18; 6:1-15; 6:15-21; 9:1-44; 11:1-44) which point to the new age of redemption achieved through the Word made flesh. The first of the signs is at Cana in Galilee (Jn 2:1-11). The final and most dramatic sign, is about to take place. Jesus goes to the tomb of Lazarus and instructs the stone to be removed. In a simple and dramatic way, Jesus declares, "Lazarus, come out!" (Jn 11:42). At the words of Jesus, who is the resurrection and the life (Jn 11:25), Lazarus emerges from the tomb. He is still encased in the burial cloth, a reminder that Lazarus will die again in the natural course of being human. But for now, Jesus instructs that Lazarus be untied and set free (Jn 11:44).

The raising of Lazarus is a sign, the greatest of the seven

signs, but a sign nonetheless. A deeper reality is indicated, the resurrection of Jesus who will never die again. Jesus' death and resurrection is the hope of all humanity being untied and set free from sin and death. The raising of Lazarus is a sign which points to the resurrection of Jesus which will make possible our coming into eternal life. Martha's profession of faith is realized in her presence. "I have come to believe that you are the Messiah, the Son of God, the one who is coming into the world" (Jn 11:27).

Kill Him

The greatest of the signs is met by the deepest of ironies. The raising of Lazarus to life evokes the final solution about Jesus— "kill him" (Jn 11:53). All of the religious authorities gather in order to put an end to Jesus. The Jews are beginning to believe in Jesus in greater numbers, especially after the raising of Lazarus (Jn 11:45). The authorities are growing increasingly concerned about the reaction of Rome which might "come and take away both our land and our nation" (Jn 11:48). The Sanhedrin (the whole of the religious authorities) makes the decision that Jesus must be sacrificed for the common good, in this case the nation. The ironic truth is that Jesus will be sacrificed for the salvation of the world.

Jesus is no religious idealist oblivious to the dangers of his public ministry, especially in Jerusalem. The shadow of the cross has never been so close. Even now the authorities are looking for someone who might hand him over. Perhaps there is one in the inner circle who could be tempted to sacrifice Jesus for "the good" of the nation (Mt 26:14-16). With each passing day, the pressure increases on Jesus; and so also ever closer the impending hour when he will reveal the depth of his love. Jesus will reveal the name of the Father (Jn 13:1). And that name is SUFFERING, ENDURING LOVE (Jn 17:26).

PRAYER

O Lord, every day we come to you with our many
needs. Very often they appear to us as
life and death concerns. We come to you in
prayer and demand an immediate response.
We want you to act on our request... now. We
take your delays as indifference or rejection.
Too often we become despondent. We give up.
We try to do everything on our own.

O Lord, give us the Holy Spirit that we might
discern your holy will in all things.
Give us the wisdom to see that you always
answer our prayers. The wisdom of your
ways is such as to always help us grow
in faith and be matured in love.
Each need is a way our loving Father uses
to elicit from us faith in his goodness.

O Lord, we must admit that we are often like
Martha. We want you to do our will.
We want you to answer our prayers. Do not delay.
There is an edge to our prayers. There is an
impatience in our voice. Calm us, O Lord. Give
us your Spirit. Replace our doubt with faith.

O Lord, let us be like Martha in our
testimony of faith. Let us live each day with
the sure knowledge that you are the resurrection
and the life. Call us forth, that we might rise from the dead.

Reflection Questions

1. What was your initial reaction to Jesus' delay before going
   to be with Martha and Mary? Were you able to identify

with Martha's anger over Jesus' delay? What might you have said to Jesus?

2. How do you respond when God does not answer your prayers immediately? Or in the way you desire? Are you able to see a deeper meaning in God's loving plan for your life?

3. In what ways has Jesus called you to move from death to life? Were you able to accept Jesus' call to come from the tomb of the past with its lack of hope? How were you able to accept Jesus' call to new life? Did you experience hostility because you followed Jesus? How? Were you able to confront this hostility?

He Withdrew

The present is prologue; what is now was once yet to be. This is certainly true when it comes to Jesus. In the opening of the Fourth Gospel, the Prologue (Jn 1:1-18), we read: "He came to what was his own but his own people did not accept him" (1:11). When Jesus returns to his hometown synagogue in Nazareth to teach, the people "rose up, drove him out of town, and led him to the brow of the hill on which their town had been built, intending to hurl him down headlong" (Lk 4:29). Now with the final sign, the raising of Lazarus, the reaction of the Sanhedrin can hardly be a surprise: "From that day on they planned to kill him" (Jn 11:53). This response by the religious authorities in Jerusalem is just what Peter wanted Jesus to avoid. The echo of Caesarea Philippi still resonates in our ears: "Then Peter took him aside and began to rebuke him, 'God forbid, Lord! No such thing shall ever happen to you'" (Mt 16:22). Perhaps we can hear Simon Peter muttering under his breath, "I told you so."

In any case, the final days of Jesus' public ministry are anything but successful as the world understands success. The Gospel of John does not try to "spin" the situation so Jesus ends up looking good. There is a stark evaluation which does not surprise and cannot be avoided: "So Jesus no longer walked about in public among the Jews..." (Jn 11:54). The situation is simply too dangerous. More to the point, it is Jesus who will determine the outcome of this long, bitter, and intense conflict. Jesus is in control of events right up to the end. No one can take Jesus' life against his will. Jesus, ever the Good Shepherd, freely lays down his life out of love for all who believe in him (Jn 10:1-18).

While we can't go home again and certainly Jesus couldn't return to Nazareth, during times of trouble we return to our base. We try to calm the turbulence of events by finding the familiar, especially returning to the arena where we knew success. So it is with Jesus. He can no longer go public with his message. The members of the Sanhedrin are determined to kill him. Jesus leaves "for the region near the desert" (Jn 11:54).

The very mention of the desert evokes all kinds of images and feelings. As a prelude to the public ministry, Jesus was led by the Spirit into the desert (Lk 4:1). It was there, after forty days of fasting and prayer, that Satan came to tempt Jesus. At the end of Jesus' time of testing, he emerged victorious and "angels came and ministered to him" (Mt 4:11). According to the Fourth Gospel, John the Baptist sets the stage for the public ministry of Jesus by his preaching "in Bethany across the Jordan" (Jn 1:28). Jesus will emerge from the wilderness as the one who will replace John's baptism of water with fire and the Holy Spirit (Mt 3:11). Finally, it is just before the raising of Lazarus during the Feast of Dedication that a bitter confrontation with the religious authorities took place (Jn 10:22-39). The authorities tried to stone Jesus as well as arrest him. Both tactics failed. Once again Jesus retreats "back across the Jordan to the place where John first baptized..." (Jn 10:40). The desert, the edge of the wilderness, is a place where Jesus often returns during times of conflict. The desert is not only a place of lifelessness and the home of Satan, it is also the place of prayer and solitude. Jesus returns to the edge of the wilderness to be renewed for the next phase of his journey to Jerusalem.

With the latest confrontation over the raising of Lazarus, a new level of determination has set in among the authorities. Plans for killing Jesus are finalized. Hence, it is very much in keeping with Jesus' response to such confrontations that he would retreat to the desert, "to a town call Ephraim" (Jn 11:54). Jesus will need all the strength he can summon for his final appearance in Jerusalem.

The message and mission given to Jesus by the Father is uniquely his as the Beloved Son to whom we should listen (Mk 1:9-11; Mt 17-5). At the same time, Jesus calls disciples to share in ministry for the Kingdom of God (Mk 1:16-20). Hence, it is not surprising that with this latest retreat to Ephraim, Jesus would remain there "with his disciples" (Jn 11:54). Soon after Jesus begins his public ministry of preaching the Kingdom, he selects his disciples. The journey to Jerusalem is never done alone. We need companions for the journey. The disciples are not perfect. They often lack understanding and prove themselves to be human, all too human. The disciples are subject to all the temptations and fears that plague the human condition. Nonetheless, Jesus calls them to follow him (Mt 4:19). In their weakness, they still found the strength to leave "their nets" and boats and families in order to see where Jesus stayed (Jn 1:37-40). No matter how frustrated Jesus became with the disciples, they were his own "and he loved them to the end" (Jn 13:1).

Preparations are well under way for the feast of the Passover. The proper place for worship is the holy city of Jerusalem. Yet also at work is the plan to arrest Jesus should he appear on the scene. Jesus calls his disciples to inform them about his plans for the Passover. It is a moment of high anxiety. Will Jesus indicate they are going to Jerusalem? Will *we* go to Jerusalem as well?

PRAYER

O Lord, as we face the challenges of living
your Gospel in our everyday life, we have
come to know the hostility of the world. We
are tempted to turn from your ways
and seek the approval of others.

O Lord, let us seek your solitude;
let us find you in holy silence.

Let us hear your word in our prayer.
We do not want to flee from
our obligation to witness to your goodness.
We want to sing out your goodness,
so that others may come to give you glory.

O Lord, bless your Church, that community
of faith, which you left behind as
the sign which points to the Kingdom. We
need the Church. We need the support
of others as we struggle to live the
life of the Spirit. We cannot do it by
ourselves. We cannot journey to Jerusalem
alone. We need fellow pilgrims to
share our burdens and strengthen our faith.

You give us good companions. Help us to
use the gifts of the Spirit to strengthen your
Church. Let us join with others to do the
work of the Kingdom. Let your mission be ours.

Reflection Questions

1. In what ways have you experienced the hostility of others in living the Gospel? Did you find it necessary to withdraw from your friends? A job? A club? How has this experience allowed you to grow closer to Jesus?
2. Do you turn in solitude to Jesus when faced with rejection and hostility for doing what is just? How has the Lord been a rock and strength for you? Were you tempted to despair? How did God's grace turn your despair into hope?
3. In what ways has the Church been a source of spiritual strength for your journey to Jerusalem? How have you helped others in their faith-journey? Did this ministry to others also help you in your life? How?

Will He Come To The Feast?

It is no longer a secret—Jesus is at the top of the Sanhedrin's most wanted list. So intense is the hostility that Jesus must withdraw from public view. However, the Passover is coming and Jesus is bound to make an appearance. Certainly speculation is rampant as to whether Jesus will come to the Passover or not (Jn 11:56). The religious authorities are taking no chances. "For the chief priests and the Pharisees had given orders that if anyone knew where he was, he should inform them, so that they might arrest him" (Jn 11:57).

INTO THE WORLD

The disciples have been with Jesus for three years. They are in the town of Ephraim just outside of Jerusalem because of the plan to arrest Jesus on sight. Yet Jesus must go to Jerusalem for the Passover, his last with the disciples, so to complete the work given to him by the Father (Jn 14:24). On a human level, how difficult a decision this had to have been. Jesus knows what awaits him and those who have been with him from the beginning. The temptation is great to withdraw, avoid Jerusalem, simply come to the Passover next year. Who could blame him? It would certainly be the reasonable thing to do. However, it would not be the faithful thing to do. Jesus must reveal the name of the Father. This revelation can only be accomplished by going to the Passover. For Jesus, the sacrificial Lamb of God (Jn 1:36), will make the Father's name known on Golgotha. And the Father's name is SUFFERING, ENDURING LOVE (Jn 17:26).

Jesus knew the temptation would always be great for his beloved community to withdraw from engagement with the world. In the face of the world's hostility, a strong case can be made to seek security and let the world continue under the domination of the Evil One. Yet Jesus' whole public life has been just that—public. Even in the face of attempts to kill him, Jesus continued his journey to Jerusalem (Jn 8:31-59). Jesus did not carry on a private war with the religious authorities. He did not go about in secret with some esoteric teaching only for the select few. Rather, as Jesus says of himself in response to Annas the high priest, "I have spoken publicly to the world. I have always taught in a synagogue or in the temple area where all the Jews gather, and in secret I have said nothing" (Jn 18:20). The response by the guard to Jesus was to strike him (Jn 18:22). Such has always been the response to Jesus as the Truth about the Father—violence.

There will come a time when Jesus will leave the disciples and ascend to the Father. This will be a difficult time for "the little flock" that must remain behind. Jesus does not pray that the disciples be taken out of the world (Jn 17:15). The disciples must remain in the world so as to *continue* the work of Jesus; the work of making the Father's name known and giving glory to Jesus as the Son of God (Jn 17:16-19). They will do this by remaining in union with Jesus, the True Vine (Jn 15:1-10); through the indwelling of the Paraclete (Jn 14:15-21); and by living a life of love (Jn 13:34-35). By living in such a way, the disciples continue to witness to Jesus as the Truth (Jn 15:26-27).

In remaining in the world, the disciples must never become *of* the world. There is the world, all of creation, which God so loves that he sends his Son to redeem it through the cross (Jn 3:16). However, there is also the world which is under the influence of Satan and is in constant opposition to the Father (Jn 16:7-11). There is that world which hates Jesus as well as the disciples (Jn 15:8). There can be no compromise with this world which will be exposed for what it is, the power of evil, by Jesus on the cross; the greater power of love (Jn 12:31-32). It is only by being consecrated in the truth of Jesus that the disciples can remain in the world without being conformed to its ways (Jn 14:25-27).

THOSE WHO WILL BELIEVE

While Jesus prays for those who have been with him from the beginning, he is also mindful of "those who will believe in me through their word" (Jn 17:20). Jesus prays for *us*. We too are Jesus' own. In the particular situation of our lives, we are to *continue* the works of witnessing to the Father as Love, Jesus as the Son of God, and love for one another as the fruit of the indwelling Paraclete (Jn 14:15-17). The way in which the world comes to know Jesus in truth is through the public witness of the disciples (Jn 17:23). The union of the Trinity and its indwelling in the community of faith brings forth the glory of God (Jn 17:22). Each of us is called to help bring forth God's glory by the fraternal love we give to one another.

As with Jesus and his disciples, so it is with us, the world continues to show hostility toward all who come in his name. Persecution, rejection, and violence are the responses of the world to Jesus. The temptation is for us to flee, be silent, and simply go along with the agenda of the world in order to maintain "peace." Yet this is not peace but cowardice and a timidity which perpetuates the reign of the Evil One.

We cannot face the Evil One by ourselves. The hatred of the world is real and intense. Left to our own powers, we would surely fail. However, we are not alone. Jesus has not left us orphans (Jn 14:18). Jesus sends us the Paraclete to be with us always (Jn 14:15-16). We can continue our journey to Jerusalem and beyond. The words of Jesus are for us, "Take courage, I have conquered the world" (Jn 16:33).

O Lord, too often we are afraid to give
public witness to your Truth. We too
often deny you with a timid silence
that gives comfort to the Father of Lies.
We rationalize our fear in the name
of civility or good manners. We don't
want to seem judgmental or harsh.
In the face of violence and lies, we
find a cheap comfort in withdrawing
from speaking the Truth.

O Lord, send your Paraclete into our hearts
as the Spirit of Truth and Courage. We
need that boldness which allows us to
witness to the truth about Jesus as the
Son of God. Let us live love in the way
you showed us on Calvary. Let us
do the Truth each day so that we may
give glory to the Father.

O Lord, each day we go forth into the
world. Each day, a gift from you, we
are challenged to be disciples of Jesus. We are
to do this in the ordinary responsibilities
of our lives. In our homes, schools, businesses,
and associations let us be of courage.
Let us share in the same courage which
you showed in overcoming the world.

Reflection Questions

1. In what ways have you been called on to give public witness to Jesus? How did you respond to such situations? Did

you face opposition? How? Did you receive support? In what ways?

2. Have you ever experienced fear in being challenged for your faith? How did prayer help you to face the challenge? How have you failed in giving public witness to Jesus? Have you experienced the forgiveness of Jesus?

3. Have you found yourself at times following the way of the world? How? What was the motivation for following the pressure of others to turn from Jesus? What lessons did you learn from these negative experiences? Have you been able to use these experiences to help others? How?

The Son Of Man

There is an essential loneliness at the center of our humanity. No matter how many or how deep the intimacy of our relationships, there is a mystery which human love cannot penetrate. There always remains a curtain which no friendship or union can part. The loneliness, the mystery, of our humanity drives us to seek understanding. There are moments, all too fleeting, when we feel that we are known. The word or gesture of a friend or a spouse can seem like a grace beyond the bounds of the natural. We are elevated, lifted up, to a point where we are seen for who and what we really are. In these moments of grace, the inner loneliness of our humanity is replaced with a sense of being at one with all that is—the look of a friend, the touch of a lover, the smile of a stranger, the tear of sorrow and joy, the taste of bread and wine, a word of comfort and challenge, the first rays of day and the velvet of night—all draw us into a deeper web of existence in which grace builds upon nature. We are made for truth, and we want to know the truth of our humanity.

Jesus, in his humanity, experienced this desire to be understood. Consider the episode between Jesus and Philip, one of the most poignant between Jesus and one of his disciples. Jesus indicates that he is the way, truth and life which leads to the Father. In fact, Jesus and the Father are one. To see Jesus is to see the Father. The work given to Jesus by the Father is just that— to make the Father known. Philip responds to Jesus by saying, "Master, show us the Father, and that will be enough for us" (Jn 14:8). The words of Jesus are filled with frustration, hurt, and loneliness. "Have I been with you for so long a time and you still do not know me, Philip? Whoever sees me has seen the Father. How can you say, 'Show us the Father'? Do you not believe that I am in the Father and the Father is in me?" (Jn 14:9-10). Jesus concludes on a plaintive note, by imploring the disciples to believe in him if for no other reason than the works he has accomplished (Jn 14:11). Right up to the end, Jesus is denied the consolation of friends who understand. In coming days, the disciples will be scattered as Jesus is arrested, put on trial, and crucified. But Jesus is never completely alone, because the Father is with him always (Jn 16:32-33).

A Tapestry Of Images

While each human being is unique, we know there are men and women who seemed to be marked out, destined for extraordinary deeds, good and evil. Often such individuals are misunderstood and lonely. Those who profoundly influence world history are complex characters, and they cannot be neatly placed in a simple category or profile. Jesus' effects on human history and human nature are beyond our poor powers of comprehension. Jesus certainly experienced his share of misunderstanding and loneliness. There is no one Gospel image that emerges to capture the essence of Jesus. We must rely on a tapestry of images and a series of titles if we are to gain some insight into Jesus.

The Gospels contain a number of titles in telling the story of Jesus: Son of God (Mk 15:39); Lamb of God (Jn 1:29); Logos (Jn 1:14); and Son of Man (Mt 17:9). The Fourth Gospel also speaks about Jesus as the Good Shepherd (Jn 10:11); the gate (Jn 10:9); and the True Vine (Jn 15:1). All of these contribute in a significant way to our understanding of Jesus. However, Jesus is always greater than any one of these titles or images. Jesus is more than all of them combined. Yet one title is most significant, that of "Son of Man." It is the one most frequently used by Jesus in speaking of himself. This title, "Son of Man," itself contains a number of functions which add to the complexity of Jesus. The Son of Man enjoys a unique relationship with God which gives his teaching an authority beyond that of the scribes (Mt 7:29). The Son of Man is able to act in ways which go beyond the confines of prescribed cultic practice as Lord of the Sabbath (Lk 6:5), and the Son of Man is the great eschatological figure who comes to judge individuals and nations at the end of the world (Mt 25:31-46; Lk 21:25-28).

A Figure Within The Tapestry

The title "Son of Man" indicates more than power and glory. The Son of Man is also a figure of poverty and detachment, lacking even the basic necessity of having a place "to rest his head" (Mt 8:20). Above all, the Son of Man is a figure of rejection, division, and opposition. On numerous occasions, Jesus tells the disciples that the Son of Man must be "handed over to the chief priests and the scribes, and they will condemn him to death and hand him over to the Gentiles who will mock him, spit upon him, scourge him, and put him to death; but after three days, he will rise" (Mk 10:33-34).

Within the Gospel tapestry of Jesus, there emerges a "figure within" (Henry James). It is the complex, demanding figure of Jesus as the One who comes out of love to do the work of the Father—love the world into reconciliation with the One alone who is Life. Yet the world loves darkness and rejects the Light of truth. The world pronounces its judgment on Jesus—the cross. However, the Father raises the Son through the power of their Spirit. It is this Figure in the Tapestry who comes to us and says, "Follow me." Have we not been with Jesus enough to know The Way? (Jn 14:1-6).

PRAYER

O Lord, we have been with you throughout
the season of Lent. We have come with you
to the holy city of Jerusalem. Our journey
has been anything but smooth. Our faith
is often weak. We falter. We have even
tried to keep you from your mission.
Yet Lord, we are in Jerusalem with you.

Throughout our journey you have told us
that the Son of Man must be rejected, suffer,
and die at the hands of the elders. We
didn't listen. We failed to understand
that you were speaking about yourself. We
didn't want to know.

O Lord, we must admit that following you
as the Son of Man meant glory and power
for us. We had visions of your coming
to judge the nations. We see ourselves
sitting on thrones judging others. Too often,
we accepted your invitation in hope
of power, not your glory.

O Lord, help us to see that you must be
rejected and put to death. Help us to
accept such a baptism. Let us drink from
the same cup of suffering.
Jesus, you are the Son of Man who must suffer
and die. You are also the One who raises us to new life.

Reflection Questions

1. Have you been able to combine Jesus as the Son of Man
   who comes in glory and the Son of Man who must be rejected and die? How? Do you see in the life of Jesus the way

both of these are present? What are some examples? What do they contribute to your spiritual life?

2. How do you see the Church living out both aspects of Jesus, that is, Suffering Servant and the One who sits at the right hand of the Father? Do you find the Church struggling to unite both aspects of Jesus? Which aspect do you think is most evident today? Why?

3. Do you find yourself worrying about the end of the world? Why? What images come to your mind when someone talks about Jesus returning in glory? On what basis will Jesus judge the nations? Each individual?

Some Greeks

It seems so long ago, that first sign at the wedding in Cana. Jesus was reluctant to act, even at the request of his mother. As he tells Mary, "My hour has not yet come" (Jn 2:4). The time and place for Jesus to reveal the glory of the Father was not at a wedding in Galilee. The supreme hour of revelation will take place on the cross at Golgotha (Jn 19:28). Of course, the entire public ministry is a process of coming into his hour. With Jesus' entry into Jerusalem, the hour is near at hand.

Jerusalem was teeming with visitors and worshipers for the Passover. Jesus and his disciples are among the throng, even though the authorities are looking to arrest Jesus. Among the worshipers are some Greeks (Jn 12:20). These are probably some Gentile converts to Judaism from the surrounding Mediterranean region. The Pharisees had speculated that Jesus might have even gone among the Greeks to teach early in his public ministry (Jn 7:34-36). No matter, some Greeks go to Philip and Andrew with a request. It is not a trivial matter that these two disciples have Greek names (Jn 1:44). We must ask, What is the significance of these Greeks (non-Jewish worshipers)? Why does John include them in the Gospel at such a key moment?

When Jesus enters Jerusalem, the Judean multitudes go to him and proclaim him king (Jn 12:12). But Jesus is not only the Savior and King of the Jews, he is also the Savior of the whole world. The Lordship of Jesus is universal. Hence, when these Greeks come looking for Jesus, they are fulfilling the ironic words of the Pharisees: "Look, the whole world has gone after him" (Jn 12:19). The acknowledgment by the Judean crowds, along with the presence of the Greeks (the non-Jewish world) is an indication of the universal salvation Jesus will achieve through the cross. Jesus states this universalism clearly. "And when I am lifted up from the earth, I will draw everyone to myself" (Jn 12:32).

SIR, WE WOULD LIKE TO SEE JESUS

The presence of the Greeks at this point in the journey to Jerusalem is crucial, for their presence not only indicates the universality of salvation, but also reveals the irony and tragedy of Jesus' coming to his own. The Prologue of the Fourth Gospel prepared us for what was to take place. "He came to his own domain and his own people did not accept him" (Jn 1:11). Throughout the public ministry we know this to be true. Time and again Jesus, in word and deed, revealed the Father. Through preaching, teaching, healing, and driving out evil spirits, Jesus made present the reign of God. Through table fellowship with sinners and the rejected, Jesus ushered in the time of grace foretold by Isaiah (Is 61:1-2; Lk 4:16-22). The various signs worked by Jesus in the Gospel of John were met with opposition, disbelief, and various plots to arrest and kill him. The religious authorities remained blind in their refusal to see Jesus as the revelation of the Father. This refusal to see serves as the self-judgment against the Pharisees. For when confronted by Jesus, they claim *not* to be blind. Jesus responds, "Blind? If you were, you would not be guilty, but since you say, 'We see,' your guilt remains" (Jn 9:41). The authorities do see Jesus, yet the hardness of their hearts blinds the eye of faith.

The Prologue's indication of Jesus' being rejected by his own, also contains the realization that others did accept Jesus: "But to all who did accept him he gave the power to become children of God, to all who believe in the name of him who was born not out of human stock or urge of the flesh or will of man but of God himself" (Jn 1:12-13). The rejection of Jesus by his own will not triumph over God's plan for salvation. The Word will become flesh. The revelation of the Father will take place. The words and works will be Light and Life to the world for its redemption. Jesus will complete all that has been given him by the Father. From the cross the Spirit will be handed over to the community of faith represented by Mary and the Beloved Disciple (Jn 19:25-27). The Greeks' asking to see Jesus is a clear indication that the work of salvation is universal *and* ongoing. This does not lessen the tragedy for Israel. Jesus came as the Light of Life so that Israel would see and not walk in darkness (Jn 8:12-13). Jesus longed to hear the request made by the Greeks from the Jewish leaders as well. We would like to see Jesus. Such was not to be.

OUR REQUEST

Lent is the time for us to see Jesus. Where do we look? We find Jesus in the marrow of our everyday lives. Jesus must once again take on flesh so that we might follow him. How does Jesus come to us? The Word becomes flesh in a special way through the poor and powerless, through the blind and those in slavery to physical and spiritual forces. Jesus comes to us in our relationship, from the most intimate of family ties to those of workplace, school, and club. Jesus comes to us in the stranger who is in need. Jesus is present in the enemy whom we are challenged to transform into a friend.

Above all, if we really desire to see Jesus, we must look to the cross. The glorious vision of the transfiguration on Mount Tabor will pass away; the triumphal entry of Jesus into Jerusalem will give way to a demand for death.

What endures is the victorious love of God made visible in Jesus on the cross.

O Lord, the hour of your glorification draws
near. Like the Greeks, we want to see you.
Yet Lord, we know that throughout your
public ministry you have been revealing
yourself to us. Too often, we failed to see
you because we looked away. We
pretended to be blind. We claimed not to
understand. O Lord, our blindness
was of our own doing.

During the time of Lent, let us see you,
Jesus, in all things. Remove the film
that covers our eyes so we may see you
in the needy, poor, confused, and fearful.
Open our hearts that the Paraclete may
indwell with the truth that sets us
free about you and the Father.
Lord, free our wills to follow you.
Break the chain of sin and the power of
our past failures. With your grace,
all things are made new. We are healed.

Each day Lord, empower us to give you the
glory you share with the Father. Let us
daily do the deeds of love, by which all
will know we are your disciples.
Draw us to yourself. Yes, draw us to
the cross, so that we may share your glory.

Reflection Questions

1. During this current Lent, in what ways have you seen Jesus
   at work in your life? The lives of others? How was the cross
   of Jesus present in these experiences?

2. What have been some of events and relationships which have kept you from seeing Jesus? Have you been able to grow from these experiences? How?

3. Have you been able to help others see Jesus in their daily lives? How? Were you able to help others see Jesus during times of their personal crosses? How? Were you able to draw on your own experiences? Which experiences? How can the Sacraments of Eucharist and Penance help you to see Jesus?

Tuesday of the Fourth Week of Lent
(John 12:24-26)

The Grain Of Wheat

We have arrived at the following point in our journey toward Jerusalem. Jesus has triumphantly entered the holy city to the adulation of the crowd and the consternation of the religious authorities (Jn 12:12-19), and some Greeks have requested to see him which reflects the saving will of Jesus to draw everyone to himself (Jn 12:32). These are no small achievements. Since the temptations in the desert, Satan has continually been at work trying to keep Jesus from Jerusalem (Mt 16:21-23; Lk 4:9-11).

The difficulties facing Jesus and the disciples are not confined to the journey to Jerusalem itself. Once they arrive at the holy city, the authorities are determined to arrest Jesus and put him to death (Jn 11:55-57; Jn 11:53). This desire to stop Jesus by any means is only strengthened by "the great crowd" that goes out to welcome Jesus into Jerusalem (Jn 12:12). A smaller victory, but no less significant, is the desire of the Greeks to see Jesus (Jn 12:20-22). In the words of the Pharisees, "the whole world has gone after him" (Jn 12:19).

THE HOUR HAS COME

Jesus takes note of both events, the entry into Jerusalem and the request by the Greeks and responds, "The hour has come for the Son of Man to be glorified" (Jn 12:23). With these words a host of familiar themes and images come rushing to mind. The hour as the time of revelation is at hand in which the mysterious figure of the Son of Man, as the one who comes in power to judge the nations, is about to be made known. Perhaps all that talk by Jesus about rejection, suffering, and even death was a bit of hyperbole.

Maybe Jesus was just testing the disciples to find out who were the true believers and would bear fruit through perseverance (Lk 8:15). The triumphal entry into Jerusalem, the request by the Greeks, and now the talk of glory for the Son of Man can only mean one thing—the Father is about to give to "the little flock" of faith the Kingdom (Lk 12:32). The disciples will be sitting on thrones judging the twelve tribes of Israel.

MY SERVANT

Once again, Jesus must supply the necessary corrective to the disciples' expectations of power and glory. The reality of Jesus' passion and death lies in the not too distant future. In many ways, the public ministry of Jesus, along with their intimate times alone, was a process of preparing the disciples for his hour of glory. Yet, it is not to be the glory that comes to those who love power; but, it is to be the glory that comes to the One who reveals the power of love. The "little flock" of faith will receive the Kingdom, but it is a Kingdom born of the suffering love of Jesus on the cross. Unfortunately, the disciples did not understand this during the public ministry. Such illumination will only come with the sending of the Holy Spirit at Pentecost (Ac 2:1-36).

For now, Jesus must try once again to explain his messiahship as one that involves rejection, suffering, and death. Jesus turns to a familiar aspect of their everyday lives—a grain of wheat. Perhaps this ordinary, everyday aspect can be used to speak of the deepest of mysteries.

The grain of wheat can only complete its task by being placed in the earth. The burial of the single grain, in effect its death, yields a rich harvest. In nature we see the mystery of life proceeding from death. And not only that, but an abundance of life. So it is with Jesus. Through his being received into the earth, his real *human* death, he brings forth the abundant life. The buried grain of wheat produces a rich harvest for the bread that will feed the hungry. The crucified and buried Jesus will rise as that "bread of life" who feeds everyone who comes to him in faith (Jn 6:51). Unlike the natural bread which feeds only the body, the bread that Jesus *is*, and gives, nourishes the whole person for life eternal (Jn 6:58). The mystery of the Christian life, in dying we are reborn and in losing our lives we gain eternal life, comes to *all* disciples. There can be no authentic following of Jesus without falling into the earth and dying to self. So often, we want a discipleship which yields an abundant harvest without the costly grace of self-denial. We want to love Jesus but all the while continue to love the world. Yet we cannot serve two masters. Only in serving Jesus does the Father honor us with eternal life (Jn 12:26).

Wherever I Am

Lent is our time of grace as we grow in discipleship and servanthood. We need to be where Jesus is. Throughout his public ministry, Jesus showed us where to find him. "I tell you solemnly, insofar as you did this to one of the least of these, you did it to me" (Mt 25:40). We are to find Jesus in the grain of wheat which dies and brings forth the harvest of eternal life. We too must be present to the least among us, and die daily to ourselves so as to be reborn into eternal life.

Prayer

O Lord, once again you speak to us of your
glory. Once again our minds race to images
of power and privilege. Again, we understand
everything in earthly terms. These quickly
fade and pass into nothingness. Your word
alone is eternal.

You offer us a new image, at once small
and familiar. You tell us to understand
your glory in terms of the grain of wheat.

Again we are confused. The grain of wheat
is a passing thing. It is placed in the earth
and dies. What glory is there in such
a fate? What lesson are we to learn?

Perhaps Lord, we struggle so much to
understand because we want to hold on to
our lives. We love our life in and for this
world. Yet you tell us, that in dying
like the grain of wheat, we pass to life eternal.
You tell us we must let go in order
to receive. We must lose in order to win.
We must die in order to know life.

Lord, you know we are afraid. How can we
be sure that we will rise? How do we
know that in falling into the earth, the harvest
of life will be reaped? By your word.
Where you are, we can go with confidence.
Strengthen our weakness.

Reflection Questions

1. What images come to your mind when Jesus speaks of his
   hour of glory? Where in the Scriptures do these images
   come from? How do these initial images of yours compare
   and contrast with the grain of wheat?
2. What are some contemporary images or symbols that
   might be used to express Jesus' hour of glory as dying and
   rising? Do you have trouble relating to pastoral images
   (sheep for example) as well as the image of the grain of
   wheat or the mustard seed? Why? Should we use more
   urban images? Can we do so without violating Scripture?
3. What experiences have drawn you into the mystery of dying to self in order to live a new life of love? How did you
   overcome your fear with such experiences? In what ways
   did you find Jesus in these experiences?

A Voice From The Sky

The magnitude of suffering that awaits Jesus is pressing in on him. The climactic showdown with Satan is not years, but only days away. The image of the grain of wheat is not simply the use of an image to teach a lesson. The grain of wheat contains existential power, that is, it speaks to and reveals the situation of Jesus. It also speaks of what is demanded of the disciples and "for those also who through their words will believe in me" (Jn 6:20). It speaks of what is demanded of us.

In the Fourth Gospel, there is no agony in the Garden. There is no sweating of blood (Lk 22:44), no angel to comfort and strengthen (Lk 22:44); and there is no request by Jesus to let his cup of suffering pass away (Mt 26:39). Even less is there any mention of a "sudden fear… and great distress" (Mk 14:33). Yes, Jesus is troubled in his soul (Jn 12:27). But this "troubling" is not a cause for panic but a necessary step in the hour of glorification. Jesus asks in a rhetorical fashion, "What shall I say: 'Father, save me from this hour?'" (Jn 12:27). From a wide variety of motives, this is exactly what others have been trying to do—have Jesus "be saved" from this hour. Satan early on tempted Jesus to display his identity apart from Jerusalem. Peter wanted to keep Jesus from the rejection, suffering, and death that awaited him (and spare himself as well). The humanity of Jesus is captured by the Fourth Gospel in his being troubled. However, he refuses to give in to Satan as well as the "concern" of Simon Peter. Jesus will not ask the Father to save him from this hour. The humanity of Jesus is not the cause for giving in to temptation. Rather, it is through his humanity that Jesus will triumph in this hour of glorification.

The response to Jesus' example of triumph over being troubled does not come from an angel (Lk 22:43), but from the Father. "I have glorified [His name] and will glorify it again" (Jn 12:28). There is a "double portion" of glory at work. Jesus has given glory to the Father throughout his public ministry, and the Father has glorified Jesus throughout that ministry. The Father and the Son are one in glory (Jn 10:1). There is also a further glory, namely, the glorification which is from the cross, and is completed when Jesus returns to the Father (Jn 16:28).

The voice from the sky is the Father's voice, but it is not heard in order to testify about Jesus. Jesus' own word and work validate who he is and the truth of his message. Rather, Jesus indicates that "this voice did not come for my sake but for yours" (Jn 12:30). The very voice of the Father is needed in order to help the crowd come to the truth, for we see that they continue to be confused and lack understanding. The crowd speculates that the voice belongs to an angel or is thunder (Jn 12:29). The inability to comprehend persists, even as the hour of glory unfolds.

Now Is The Time Of Judgment

From the perspective of the Fourth Gospel, the hour, the time of glorification and judgment, is *now*. There is not some later and more convenient hour for the glory of God to be revealed. The Father's glory is revealed in the ministry and cross of Jesus. Granted, the glory of God will be completed with the return of Jesus to the Father, but the process of revealing God's glory is in the here and now.

Likewise with judgment, Jesus proclaims, "Now is the time of judgment on this world; now the ruler of this world will be driven out" (Jn 12:31). The public ministry is about to conclude. Jesus has publicly made known the name of the Father in word and deed. Judgment is now. Each person who hears Jesus is called to make a *decision*. The judgment Jesus brings is always a *self*-judgment. For Jesus is not sent to condemn the world but to save it (Jn 3:17). When one hears Jesus, the time of judgment is now. To believe in Jesus is to experience eternal life—now. To persist in unbelief is to perish. But the judgment which comes is based on the free decision one makes in response to Jesus. "Whoever believes in him will not be condemned, but whoever does not believe has already been condemned, because he has not believed in the name of the only Son of God" (Jn 3:18).

THE RULER OF THIS WORLD

Satan, the ruler of this world, has from the beginning tried to keep Jesus from Jerusalem. We now see clearly why this was so important. The ruler of this world will be driven out, defeated, "...when I [Jesus] am lifted up from the earth" (Jn 12:32). The defeat of Satan comes at the very moment when he seems to have won; the hour of the cross. To the world, under the rule of Satan, the cross is the defeat of Jesus. To the eye of faith, the cross is the supreme victory over Satan (1 Cor 1:18-25).

So it comes to us miles and generations removed, but no less real and urgent. We must enter into our own time of judgment. We have traveled with Jesus throughout Lent to the holy city of Jerusalem. We too have heard the words, seen the mighty deeds, and witnessed the power of that evil in opposition to Jesus. We have also seen the power of the Kingdom to heal and drive out evil spirits. Hence, the time for a decision is now. And the decision is ours.

PRAYER

O God, you speak to us from heaven about
your Son, and our Redeemer, Jesus.
You tell us that he is the One sent in the
flesh to show your love. For, Lord, it is
not enough for us to hear your word. We
must see the Word. We must be touched

in our hearts by the Word made flesh. There
is healing in your reaching down into
our condition, so that we might be raised
up to be your reconciled people.

Yet, God, we continue in our confusion. We
still live with a shallow faith that
does not dare venture out into the deep
waters of life. Help us to surrender
our doubts and face our fears. Help
us to leave all that we hold dear,
and each day give glory to Jesus as Lord.

O Lord, through Baptism we are called to
give Jesus glory. This means we must
again remember the grain of wheat. We must
go into the earth. We must die to ourselves.
We must be reborn in the likeness of your
Son, and our Savior. All this is too
wonderful for us. Our resources are meager. With
you, all things are possible.

Reflection Questions

1. In what ways have you felt God speaking to you? How
   have you responded? How has prayer helped you discern
   God's will for you? Do you have a spiritual director? Has
   this been helpful? How?
2. In what ways have you been able to give glory to Jesus
   during this Lenten season? Have you been closed to God's
   word for your life? About Jesus? Why? How have you tried
   to be more open to God's voice?
3. What do you think Jesus is challenging the Church to be
   in the new millennium? How can the Church go about answering this call? How can your local parish be a part of
   God's work? How can *you* be faithful to your baptismal call
   to give God glory?

They Refused To Believe

The Fourth Gospel contains a number of Jesus' discourses. The first of these discourses (a dialogue which becomes a monologue) is between Jesus and a Pharisee named Nicodemus (Jn 3:1). The power of its truth reaches to illuminate the public ministry of Jesus. It also helps us to appreciate the significance of the completion of Jesus' ministry. Jesus' dialogue with Nicodemus began with a discussion about being "born again" (Jn 3:4). The dialogue, in usual Johannine fashion, becomes a monologue in which Jesus reveals *why* he was sent by God (the Father). "For God did not send his Son into the world to condemn the world, but that the world might be saved through him. Whoever believes in him will not be condemned, but whoever does not believe has already been condemned, because he has not believed in the name of the only Son of God" (Jn 3:17-18). Hence, at the closing of his public ministry we find Jesus making one last effort, out of saving love, to evoke faith in response to him.

Once again Jesus turns to a familiar pair of opposites, namely, light and darkness (Jn 12:35-36). In an urgent tone, Jesus calls the crowd to "walk while you have the light" (Jn 12:35). Jesus, the light, is soon to depart (Jn 12:35). Jesus will be "lifted up" on the cross, and he will return to the Father to share "the glory that I had with you before the world began" (Jn 17:5). As the light recedes from view, darkness is spreading and threatens to overcome those who refuse to believe (Jn 2:11). Yet Jesus refuses to give up hope. The darkness, the domain loved by Satan, will not triumph. Jesus, the light, "shines in the darkness, and the darkness has not overcome it" (Jn 1:5). Even though the light will be with them only a little longer and the darkness is spreading, Jesus still offers the hope of salvation by making it possible for them to become "children of the light" (Jn 12:36; 1 Th 5:5; Eph 5:8-14).

HE HID FROM THEM

The final decision for belief or unbelief must be decided by each person in the sacred solitude of his or her own being. Jesus has offered one last invitation to walk in the truth of the light and not be overcome by darkness (Jn 12:35). With this final offer of grace his public ministry comes to a close (Jn 12:36). Once before, Jesus withdrew from the crowd. After the raising of Lazarus, the Sanhedrin made plans to kill Jesus. As a result, "Jesus no longer walked about in public among the Jews" (Jn 11:54). He would return from his triumphal entry into Jerusalem (Jn 12:12), and this subsequent last encounter with the crowd, inviting them to believe in him (Jn 12:35-36). This time there is a finality. "Jesus left and hid from them" (Jn 12:36). The public ministry has concluded. The next time Jesus is seen in public, it will be as the rejected *and* glorified Son of Man lifted up on the cross (Jn 12:32; Jn 19:19).

With the close of his public ministry, Jesus turns to his disciples, his own from the beginning, and whom he has loved till the end (Jn 13:1). Jesus' final words, his last will and testament, will be for and with those whom he no longer calls servants but friends (Jn 15:15). Yet in a profound way, Jesus' words transcend the intimate setting of that last Passover (Lk 22:15) and speak to "those who will believe in me through their word" (Jn 17:20). Jesus is speaking to us. But before entering that intimate circle of friends, we must take one last look at the public ministry of Jesus (Jn 12:37).

There is a stark directness that is offered at the end of his public ministry: "…they refused to believe in him" (Jn 12:37). Jesus spoke the truth about the Father. Jesus performed "many signs" in their midst. Yet at the end of the ministry, there is no escaping the fact that the unbelief of the people must be acknowledged. The words of the Prologue have come to pass, "To his own he came, yet his own did not accept him" (Jn 1:11). There is no attempt to put a positive "spin" on the unbelief of the people and authorities. Reality must be faced. Consolation is not in terms of worldly success, but Jesus' victory comes in being faithful to the work given him by the Father. Because of Jesus' faithfulness, the Father loves the Son and bestows on him the glory they shared from the beginning (Jn 17:24-26).

Every disciple of Jesus must face the rejection of the world. Our best efforts and sincerest attempts at speaking the truth about Jesus can be met with unbelief. We are tempted to abandon the mission. We can give in to self-righteousness. Yet this is not the way of Jesus. Even in the face of unbelief, Jesus continues to offer the opportunity for conversion. No matter how late in the day, as long as the light is still shining, there is hope of belief. We must continue to walk in the light of Christ. For we know where we are going. We move ever closer to Golgotha. We are called to be part of the figures around the cross.

PRAYER

O Lord, you came as the Word to reveal the
very nature of God. You came in the flesh
so that we might be restored to our true
humanity. What sin obscured, you brought
to light. What rebellion lost, your restored by
your life of obedient love. Our banishment
was reversed by your calling us to be
children of the heavenly Father.

O Lord, your public ministry was one of
doing the will of the Father. You did this
work completely and always with complete love.
Let us follow your example. We too
are called, by Baptism, to do the will of our
heavenly Father. Help us to do it with love.

Jesus, you are the Light of the World. You are
the Light which leads to eternal life.
Too often we walk in the dark. We know
our deeds are sinful. We fear the
judgment you bring. Yet, Lord, we
know that you do not judge us. We
judge ourselves by what we say and do.
Above all, the judgment that we receive
comes from our response to you.
Help us each day to walk with
you, the true Light, that brings salvation.

Reflection Questions

1. In what ways have you walked by the light of Christ this
   Lent? How has the darkness of sin tried to keep you from
   following Jesus? Were you able to overcome these temptations? How?
2. How would you evaluate the public ministry of Jesus?
   What do you consider to be his most important sign,
   miracle, or teaching? What was the reaction of the crowd?
   What do you think was Jesus' greatest disappointment?
   Why?
3. What are some important disappointments in your own
   ministry of following Jesus? How did the Lord use those
   disappointments to help you grow into deeper forms of
   loving service? How has disappointment helped you draw
   closer to Jesus?

I Did Not Come To Condemn

The temptation to condemn those who do not agree with us or appreciate our insights is quite common. We have labored at some project only to have it rejected by our superiors or colleagues. From the best of intentions, we want to help others; but, they refuse our aid. We have even shown others that our plans will work, yet we are attacked on a personal level or our motives are questioned. In the end, we experience a good deal of frustration. We simply want to walk away and let the destruction occur. There are times when we even want to bring about destruction in order to punish those who are blind.

The human reaction to rejection is seen in the disciples, James and John. Jesus, on his way to Jerusalem, had to pass through a Samaritan town. However, they did not welcome him. At that point, James and John made the following suggestion to Jesus. "Lord, would you not have us call down fire from heaven to destroy them?" (Lk 9:54). Tempting. Such is not the way of Jesus. Saint Luke does not tell us precisely what Jesus said to "the sons of thunder." The Gospel simply indicates that Jesus "turned toward them only to reprimand them" (Lk 9:55). Even more to the point, Jesus and the disciples "set off for another town" (Lk 9:56). In other words, the need to reach Jerusalem and complete the work given to Jesus by the Father would not be delayed by petty inhospitality. Besides, displays of divine retribution are contrary to Jesus as the Compassion and Jubilee of the Father. Jesus is the one who searches for the lost sheep and the misplaced coin (Lk 15:1-10). The heavenly Father of Jesus is the God who rushes from the house when he catches sight of the prodigal son

(Lk 15:11-32). Jesus came to send down the fire of the Holy Spirit which renews hearts and not flames of destruction.

As we have seen, the public ministry closed on a note of disappointment: "Despite his many signs performed in their presence, they refused to believe in him" (Jn 12:37). No doubt Jesus, in his humanity, felt frustration and sadness. Perhaps once again some of his disciples are urging a divine display of destructive forces. Yet to do such a thing would be contrary to the entire purpose of his public ministry. To give in to destruction and condemnation would clearly indicate the ministry had failed. But it would have been Jesus' failure as much as the blindness of those who refused to see and believe. Jesus' words of long ago come once again to mind. "God did not send the Son into the world to condemn the world, but that the world might be saved through him" (Jn 3:17). Now at the close of his public ministry, Jesus once again proclaims his mission as one of salvation not condemnation. "I did not come to condemn the world but to save it" (Jn 12:47).

THE WORD AS JUDGE

Jesus refuses to be our judge so that we might not play the role of victim and fall into self-pity. Jesus' refusal to be our judge does not relieve us of responsibility. We must make a decision of belief or unbelief about Jesus and the word he reveals. This is the most radical and demanding call to personal responsibility and accountability. We hear the word. We know the mighty works of Jesus. The decision falls squarely to us, belief in Jesus as the Son of God or unbelief in the One who is before us. In effect, it is we who judge ourselves. The basis for our self-judgment is the word of truth spoken by Jesus. "Whoever rejects me and does not accept my words already has his judge, namely, the word I have spoked—it is that which will condemn him on the last day" (Jn 12:48). What is even more crucial is the source of the words spoken by Jesus. Jesus does not proclaim himself or make up his own message. Jesus faithfully proclaims what he was instructed by the Father. Hence, to accept or reject the words of Jesus is to accept or reject the Father (Jn 12:49). The reason Jesus does not vary from or alter the words of the Father is because the word of the Father bestows "eternal life" (Jn 12:50). When we accept or reject the words of Jesus, we are pronouncing judgment on ourselves. To accept the words of Jesus is to know eternal life. To reject the words of Jesus is to bring eternal damnation upon ourselves (Jn 14:10-11).

LIGHT OF THE WORLD

The Bible begins with the story of creation. The first act of creation through the word of God is light. "Let there be light" (Gn 1:3). The contrast to light is the darkness of sin. This is the domain of Satan, the Father of Lies. The story of human history is one of conflict between light and darkness, truth and falsehood. The conflict finds its way into the human heart. It is into this conflict that Jesus comes as the Light of the World (Jn 8:12). In the Prologue of John's Gospel, the Genesis of the New Creation, the Word becomes flesh (Jn 1:14) as the true Light of the World which gives Life (Jn 1:4-5). At the same time, there is the realization that "men loved darkness rather than light because their deeds were wicked" (Jn 3:19). It is only the light of truth, made visible in Jesus, that brings eternal life.

Lent is our time of pilgrimage from darkness to light; from lies to truth which sets us free and gives life. The power of sin, the force of darkness, is strong because we are fearful our deeds will be seen in the light (Jn 3:20). We need have no such fear. For where there is perfect love, there is no fear (1 Jn 4:18). Jesus is that perfect love. Jesus drives out all fear. Jesus comes to us as Light and Life with these words, "As the Father has loved me, so I have loved you. Live in my love" (Jn 15:9).

PRAYER

O Lord, throughout your public ministry, you
proclaimed truth. You are the Light of the
World, the Light of Life. Help us each day to
walk in the light of your truth. Let us
be witnesses to you, the true Light who
shines in the darkness of sin.

O Lord, we must admit our fear of the
light. We fear the exposure that comes
with the light. For our deeds are done
in darkness because of our sins.
We fear your condemnation. We cannot
stand your judgment, just though it is.

O Lord, let your word of mercy come to
me. For you are perfect love. You drive
out all fear with the truth. We find
it all too hard to believe. We know
we deserve condemnation. Yet you were
sent out of love from the Father to
save us. You deal with us in love; the
perfect blending of justice and mercy.

O Lord, do not withdraw from us. Take not
the light of your presence from us.
For if you go, we have no hope of life.
We flounder in our weakness. We get
lost in our sin. Yet you reach out to
us in love. You are our Light of Salvation.

Reflection Questions

1. Do you find yourself wanting God to punish evil doers?
   How does this desire conform to the message of the Gospel? What do you think Jesus would say and do?

2. Have you been your own judge in following Jesus? How have you experienced Jesus' forgiving love? Were you able to accept Jesus' love and forgiveness? What obstacles did you have to overcome?

3. In what ways has Jesus, the Light of the World, helped you to see the truth? Were you afraid to know the truth? Why? In what ways have you been walking in the darkness? How have you tried to walk in the light during this Lenten season?

Praise Of Men To The Glory Of God

The public ministry has concluded with a less than positive review. We are about to lift the curtain on Jesus and the disciples as they share that first Last Supper. But before we enter the Upper Room, a nagging question continues to hound our reflections: Why did Jesus' own people refuse to believe in him? Why were the religious authorities so hostile, even to the point of having him put to death? These are not easy questions to ask or answer. Yet they are crucial as we come to the close of Jesus' public ministry. The Fourth Gospel offers us an answer which is at once theological and anthropological.

Initially, the Fourth Gospel views the rejection of Jesus as the fulfillment of the words of Isaiah. "He has blinded their eyes, and numbed their hearts, lest they see or comprehend, or have a change of heart—and I should heal them" (Is 6:9-10; Jn 12:40). As with Pharaoh during the time of the Exodus, so it is with the people of Jesus' day, there is a hardening of the heart against the ways of God (Ex 5:1). The hardening of the heart, and the blinding of the eyes, is not caused by God but permitted. Each person is responsible for the decision of belief or unbelief in response to Jesus and his words. Jesus persists in calling people from darkness to light. However, Jesus never forces anyone to put their faith in him. In fact, it is essential that each disciple freely declare their belief in Jesus. After the Bread of Life discourse in which Jesus teaches that eternal life is for those who eat his flesh and drink his blood (Jn 6:54), we are told that many who followed Jesus found these words "hard to endure!" (Jn 6:60). In the end, these followers "broke away and would not remain in his company any longer" (Jn 6:66). Finally, Jesus turns to the Twelve and asks, "Do you want to leave me too?" Simon Peter, speaking for the others, affirms their belief in Jesus. "Lord, to whom shall we go? You have the words of eternal life. We have come to believe; we are convinced that you are God's holy one" (Jn 6:67-69). The words of eternal life offered by Jesus are accepted by the words of faith spoken by Simon Peter.

Many Who Believed In Him

The disbelief of the people and the authorities goes deeper than the words of Isaiah about the hardening of the heart indicate. The hostility and rejection by Jesus' own is anthropological; that is, it is the result of a fundamental flaw in human nature. And what is this basic orientation in the human heart which rejects Jesus? It is the moral failure of the person to acknowledge Jesus because of fear and pride.

The Fourth Gospel tells us that many of the Sanhedrin believed in Jesus. Yet they would not admit this publicly. They were afraid of the Pharisees who might put them out of the synagogue (which was the case during the time of John). To put faith in Jesus as the Son of God would result in expulsion from the synagogue. This carried a great deal of social consequences. The expelled member of the synagogue would be shunned along with their family. Their places of business would suffer. There would be a general loss of status, authority, and identity within a small, tightly knit community. The pressure was enormous to publicly denounce Jesus.

This fear of expulsion is coupled with pride, that is, preferring "the praise of men to the glory of God" (Jn 12:43). We like to hear ourselves spoken well of and held in the good esteem of others. This inflates our ego and places ourselves at the center of things. In place of obedience to the will of the Father, we seek our own will. We do not submit to the Father. We do not deny ourselves, but we affirm ourselves to the exclusion of God and our neighbor (Mk 8:34-38). This attitude is the complete opposite of Jesus who "humbled himself, obediently accepting even death, death on a cross!" (Ph 2:8).

PUBLIC WITNESS

To be a true disciple of Jesus is to give *public* witness to the Light of Life. A private, well disguised belief is not acceptable. We must *do* the truth about Jesus, the truth of who Jesus is so as to continue the glorification of the Father. The pressure is great to be silent. Our culture does not welcome any public expressions of faith. Some in the Church often counsel a timid faith in the name of cooperation and fellowship. We must not, however, confuse cooperation with compromise. We must dare to be heroic by speaking the truth with love. But always we must speak the truth we are given by the Paraclete, who will guide us in all truth (Jn 16:13).

The need for public witness in the face of hostility and rejection is a great challenge for each generation of disciples. Satan, the Father of Lies, is always at work trying to extinguish the Light and silence the Truth. It is easy to rationalize our timidity as tolerance. Conformity can come to be viewed as civility. Understanding has a way of being taken as acceptance of what is wrong or untrue. It is at such times that we must give public witness to Jesus as the Way, the Truth, and the Life (Jn 14:6). We need not be afraid. For Jesus promised at such times of testing, we need not worry about what to say. "You yourselves will not be the speakers; the Spirit of your Father will be speaking in you" (Mt 10:20).

PRAYER

O Lord, too often we seek the praise of human
beings. We want to be accepted and well
received by our peers. We court the favor of
those over us. At times this calls for us to
compromise our beliefs and act contrary to what
we know is true. Lord, we are weak.

O Lord, let your Holy Spirit shine through our
human weakness. Send the Paraclete, the
Spirit of Truth, to give us the wisdom and
courage to face the darkness of sin.
The power of the world is real. Daily we
feel its presence as the pressure to be
silent in the face of injustice, to withdraw
from the struggle for righteousness, and
to be deaf to the call of conscience.

O Lord, let your attitude be ours. We are
proud and arrogant. We refuse to do the
will of the Father. We rebel against your
word which alone gives eternal life.
Let us be humble. Let us reorganize the truth
of our lives, namely, we are made for God.
Above all, O Lord, let us each day seek your
glory. Change our hardened hearts to ones
which beat with total love for you.

Reflection Questions

1. In what ways have you sought the glory of God? In what
   ways have your Lenten practices helped you in this quest?
   How have you helped others seek the glory of God? How
   did they help you in your spiritual life?
2. In what ways have you sought the praise of others rather
   than God's glory? What were the consequences of obtain-
   ing the praise of others? Did you become more prideful?
   Were you fearful of losing their respect? Did you find yourself compromising your beliefs and values? How?
3. In what ways have you been recently called upon to give
   public witness to Jesus? Were you afraid? How did you
   confront the fear? Did you sense the Holy Spirit's presence
   giving you wisdom and strength? How?

V

FIGURES AROUND THE CROSS

The road to Jerusalem has been long and winding. We have traveled with Jesus to the holy city of his baptism of fire, his cup of suffering. Along the way, we witnessed the highs and lows of the public ministry. We were deeply moved at the first preaching of the Gospel by Jesus after his victory over Satan in the desert (Mt 4:11; 4:17). We thrilled to the various miracles in which Jesus cured the sick and healed those in the grip of evil spirits (Mt 4:23; Mk 9:14-29). The compassion of Jesus toward the crowd was evident as he fed their physical *and* spiritual hunger with earthly food and the food of eternal life (Lk 15:32; Jn 6:54). We have been inspired by Jesus' courage in speaking truth to power. Jesus never compromised the message and work given him by the Father, even in the face of enormous hostility (Mt 23:1-36). We were filled with awe at the transfiguration of Jesus (Mt 17:1-8). In these best of times, Jesus was welcomed by the crowds. Their faith in him was strong, and Jesus worked many miracles among them.

As we traveled with Jesus to Jerusalem it was also a time of testing. Jesus was rejected in his home town of Nazareth (Lk 4:16-30). The disciples continually failed to understand the words and actions of Jesus. This is especially true when it came to his passion and death (Mt 16:13-23). Throughout Jesus' public ministry, his authority is challenged by the Pharisees (Mt 21:23-27). The greatest of Jesus' signs, the raising of Lazarus from the dead, becomes the very occasion for the authorities to formulate their plan to kill him (Jn 11:53). Jesus had to endure not only the rejection by his own people, but also the inhospitality of the non-Jewish population (Lk 9:51-56). Yet through all of these "worst of times," Jesus continued to preach the good news and keep his face resolute toward Jerusalem. Throughout his prophecy of the passion, Jesus always included the hope of resurrection (Lk 18:31-34).

The best of times and the worst of times resulting from the public ministry are behind us. The curtain has come down on this phase of the work given to Jesus by the Father. In these closing weeks and days of Lent, we are invited into the concluding work of the Son. We are now to enter the intimate phase of Jesus' revelation with his own, whom he loves to the end (Jn 13:1). The next time the world sees Jesus, it will be during his passion and crucifixion, his hour of glory when he draws all things to himself (Jn 12:31-32). For now the world, which does not know Jesus, will see him no more. It is with the disciples (and those who come after in faith) that Jesus will now reveal himself (Jn 14:16-18).

During the public ministry, Jesus made himself known through word and deed. Jesus revealed the Father, and will completely reveal Him on the cross. Further revelation away from the public will be for Jesus' disciples who are now the friends who share his Passion. We will also see the disciples revealed in ways as never before. The interaction between Jesus and his own is rich in revelation as to what it means to be a disciple. Jesus will make himself known as never before. The ultimate revelation of Jesus and the Father will be from the cross. It is around the cross that the very nature of the Father is revealed by Jesus.

Before we take our places on Golgotha, there is much left to see, hear, and ponder. Before we become a figure around the cross, we are invited to be a guest at the Last Supper.

A Dispute Arose

This moment has been a long time in the making; the final Passover and Last Supper shared by Jesus with those whom he loves until the end. This moment is most human. Often the key moments in our lives include eating with loved ones—a graduation; a wedding rehearsal dinner; an ordination luncheon, to name but a few. The sharing of a meal is more than a biological necessity; it is a revelation of who we are and what we hope to become. Eating with loved ones is a communion in which we express what is deepest in our souls. Table fellowship is sacramental, that is, it reveals a sacred dimension of ourselves and others.

A good supper requires preparation. A Last Supper demands even more attention to detail. Jesus sends Peter and John to make preparations for the Passover on the day of Unleavened Bread (the day on which the Passover lamb had to be sacrificed). They complete the preparations. All is in order; Jesus arrives and takes his place at the table (Lk 22:7-14).

I HAVE LONGED TO EAT THIS PASSOVER

This is no ordinary Passover. Throughout his public ministry Jesus has told the disciples of his impending passion and death in Jerusalem (Mk 9:12-13). There is a somber atmosphere which casts a pall over the celebration. There is a dread which is beginning to grip the hearts of the disciples. Finally Jesus speaks, "I have longed to eat this Passover with you before I suffer..." (Lk 22:15-16). As if the talk of suffering isn't enough, Jesus goes on to tell the disciples, "here with me on the table is the hand of the man who betrays me" (Lk 22:21). All this talk of suffering and betrayal is too much for the disciples. They began to question one another. An atmosphere of suspicion has now taken hold. The disciples all began to proclaim their innocence (Mt 26:22-23). Never one to miss an opportunity for self-promotion, Peter tells Jesus, "Even if I have to die with you, I will never disown you" (Mt 26:35).

Not only is character revealed while eating, but we can also take the measure of a person or community by observing how they respond under pressure. Hemingway once described courage as grace under pressure. That is, courage enables one to maintain a sense of purpose and direction in the face of danger. The disciples are under a great deal of pressure. Jesus is going to suffer and die. He will not share the new covenant with them "until it is fulfilled in the Kingdom of God" (Lk 22:16). There is a traitor among them. The tension is tremendous. How will they respond? What will the pressure of the occasion reveal?

ONE WHO SERVES

To Luke's credit, he does not try to cover up or "spin" what occurs at the table. He provides us with a biblical version of what might be called, "Disciples Acting Badly." Under the pressure of the occasion, and the realization of Jesus' impending demise, "a dispute arose between them" (Lk 22:24). Of course this is quite human and not uncommon during times of tension (weddings, funerals, and children leaving for college). Tempers are short. Nerves are on edge. Words are said which cannot be unsaid or put back in our throats. So it is with the disciples; these human, all too human vessels of clay.

The nature of their dispute reveals how little they have understood Jesus and his message. The dispute concerns, "which one should be reckoned the greatest" (Lk 22:24-25). We can only imagine the frustration Jesus must have felt. Nevertheless, Jesus goes about explaining once again the meaning of "greatness" in the Kingdom of God as opposed to a worldly understanding of greatness. And Jesus points to himself as the truth about being a leader.

The entire public ministry of Jesus has involved, as an essential aspect, service. Immediately following the first preaching about the Kingdom, Jesus goes about "curing all kinds of diseases and sickness among the people" (Mt 4:23). The parable of the Last Judgment depicts the Son of Man separating the saved from the condemned on the basis of service to the least of one's brothers and sisters. In fact, service to the least is actually service to and for Jesus (Mt 25:31-46). Hence, Jesus clearly connects greatness with servant-leadership: "The greatest among you... the leader... must behave... as if he were the one who serves. For who is the greater: the one at table or the one who serves?" (Lk 22:26-27). The answer of the world is clear—the one who reclines at table. Yet, Jesus tells the disciples to look to him. What do they see? "I am among you as one who serves!" (Lk 22:27). The implication is clear: be servants as well.

STAND BY ME

This dispute about greatness and leadership is motivated by many things—ambition, power, fear of abandonment, and the desire for recognition. It is this desire for recognition that prompts Jesus to address the disciples. He is aware of how much they have sacrificed. He acknowledges their fidelity during times of persecution and rejection. Jesus has not taken them for granted! They will not be forgotten. Jesus even goes to the point of conferring on them a kingdom. They will also share Jesus' Kingdom and "sit on thrones to judge the twelve tribes of Israel" (Lk 22:28-30). Yet the Kingdom that Jesus bestows is one of loving service to the point of laying down his very life. Before one can sit on a throne as judge, one must be nailed to a cross in imitation of the Suffering Servant.

But sometimes words are not enough. The examples of long ago yesterdays have lost their power to inspire. There is the need for a new, dramatic example....

PRAYER

O Lord, you have invited us to join you for this
Last Supper and Passover before you suffer.
Honestly, we simply don't know what to make
of the future. You are going away from us.
This last meal fills us with anxiety. We have come
to depend on you. We want to keep you with
us. We are fearful of the tomorrow we face by
ourselves.

O Lord, we want to live in fidelity to your
example. Help us to be servants as you
lived the life of servant-leadership. Fill our
hearts with a humility that comes from
living your truth. For it is in service to
others that we come to offer true
leadership. Greatness is found in our
ability to give to others in the measure
in which we have received from the Father's
goodness.

O Lord, let your attitude be ours. We want
to empty ourselves of that pride which
blinds us to your gifts, and the opportunity
we have to help others. Above all, we must
empty ourselves so that your Holy Spirit will
be that creative love which lights our
way. Let us see you in others, and let

us give your love by meeting the needs of
the least of our brothers and sisters.

Reflection Questions

1. How do you respond to pressure situations? Are you able to trust that God's Spirit will give you the courage to face any trial? Do you try and find ways to bring peace in place of conflict? How?

2. What ways have you been of service to others during this Lent? To your parish? To your school or business? Do you find yourself wanting to be served by others? How do you plan to be of more service in imitation of Jesus?

3. How have you been faithful to Jesus in your Christian life? What areas of weakness are in special need of God's grace? How has your Lenten spiritual program been directed to dying to self so as to be a person for others in imitation of Mary and Jesus?

He Rose From The Meal

Every parent, teacher, and coach knows there are times when words are not enough. Actions *do* speak louder than words. Jesus has reached such a point with the disciples. They have been together for three years. Jesus has taught them about the mysteries of the Kingdom (Mt 13). A wisdom hidden from the learned and the clever has been revealed to them, mere children in the faith (Mt 11:25-27). The disciples have been exposed to the teachings of Jesus, from the great synagogues to the vast fields in which large crowds gathered (Lk 4:16; Lk 21:15; Mk 8:1). They could not help but be inspired by the great things God was doing through Jesus. And yet the lessons, sermons, and words have collected a dust which now requires a cleansing. In the midst of their dispute about greatness and leadership, Jesus has called them to look at him as the one who serves. They are to do likewise. Yet the dispute rages on. The lesson is not learned. The time for action is now. It must be an action that is at once dramatic and simple; all the while, it must be perfectly ordinary, inviting them to a deeper way of discipleship.

Parable In Action

On numerous occasions, Jesus has used parables to teach the mysteries of the Kingdom of heaven (Mt 13; Jn 10; Lk 15; Mk 4). The parables of Jesus were not only used to teach a lesson, they were also employed to challenge a prevailing religious belief which had become an ideology for power or control. The Pharisees and scribes misused the Mosaic Law and their human traditions to "tie up heavy burdens and lay them on men's shoulders, but will they lift a finger to move them? Not they!" (Mt 23:4-5). Jesus also used parables to correct popular misconceptions about righteousness, moral worthiness, and relying on appearances to determine who is just and unjust (Lk 16:19-31; 18:9-14; 19:1-10). Jesus' parables, his stories, served to challenge, subvert, and correct a truth which became so absolute, as to even deny God's mercy in bringing about a conversion. The particular truth became an idol, an end in itself which left no room for grace or freedom.

In the midst of their dispute about greatness, Jesus performs a parable in action. That is, Jesus challenges and corrects the disciples' understanding of what it means to be a leader in the community of faith. The disciples believe leadership consists in giving orders and greatness is measured in terms of mighty deeds. Leaders have titles and impress everyone by their sheer presence. However, the standards of the world are not those used to judge Jesus and his beloved community. Jesus, their "teacher and master," is in their midst as one who washes feet. The "mighty deeds" that characterize the disciples of Christ must be deeds of humble service. In fact, the most menial of tasks done with love reveals true greatness. The leader is the one who is able to inspire the community to further acts of humble service. Jesus gives the disciples an example not of struggling ascent up the organizational ladder, but one of loving descent into servant leadership. The power of Jesus' real presence is found in being in their midst as one who serves. It is the real presence of that love which continues in our own time as bread and wine (Jn 6:54-56).

The disciples are stunned into silence, except for Simon Peter. Washing the feet of a guest was the most menial of tasks, assigned to the last of the least. If anything, the disciples should be washing Jesus' feet. Better yet, have someone else wash the feet of both Jesus and the disciples. Yet here is Jesus performing this most humbling of tasks. No doubt they gave one another side glances and wondered what Jesus could possibly have in mind. Well, the other disciples might submit to such a thing but not Peter. He will speak up. However, he enjoys no more success with Jesus here than he did at Caesarea Philippi when he tried to keep Jesus from going down to Jerusalem (Mt 16:21-23). Once again, Jesus must rebuke Simon Peter for his rashness (Jn 13:6-11).

Simon Peter, because he is the leader who will soon be entrusted with the keys to the Kingdom, is most in need of having his feet washed. He needs to understand what Jesus has done and the lesson he is leaving them. If Simon Peter is to be a great leader, he must be able to wash the feet of the members of the community. Peter must be able to provide such menial service so one day he can be a shepherd in imitation of the Good Shepherd (Jn 10:1-21). Indeed, one day Peter will "lay down his life for the sheep" (Jn 10:15). One day, Peter will stretch out his hands and be led where he does not want to go (Jn 21:18). One day, Peter will follow Jesus by his own crucifixion to the glory of the Father (Jn 21:19).

BLIND AMBITION

The dispute about greatness and leadership is a perennial issue for the Church. The temptation for those in authority is for personal glory and to be in the community as those who recline and expect service. The challenge is to be the servant-leader in imitation of the Jesus who washes feet. The poison released by ambition is lovelessness, the very opposite of what is to characterize the Christian community (Jn 13:35). Ambition knows no limits to the using of people for personal gain and glory. The antidote to the poison of ambition is humble service in imitation of Jesus. The only ambition that is to be found among Christians is the ambition "for the spiritual gifts" (1 Cor 12:31). And the greatest of these is LOVE (1 Cor 13:13).

Jesus speaks beyond that Passover, to those who come after in his name. Jesus speaks to us, "I have given you a model to follow, so that as I have done for you, you should also do" (Jn 13:15). In the most humble, simple acts of service we imitate Jesus. The more exalted our position, the more we are to humble ourselves. For it is in emptying ourselves that we put on the attitude of Jesus (Ph 2:5). And blessed will we be (Jn 13:17).

PRAYER

O Lord, we are at this final Passover and Last
Supper with you. We know you are about to
depart. The forces of death are gathering. We
will not have you, the Light, with us much
longer. Yet we must continue the work given
you by the Father. You entrusted this work
to us through the indwelling of the Paraclete.

O Lord, you leave us with an example that
troubles our ways of doing things. You
want us to be of service. You call us to be
humble. And you won't allow us to
avoid the challenge. You are in our midst
as Servant. Not only a servant, but
one who does the most menial of tasks.
What elevates these small services
is total love. For it is love which
elevates the most insignificant
into the realm of the divine.

O Lord, each day we have the opportunity to
be of service to others. We have the opportunity
to bring Jesus to that part of the world we
touch. We can bring the Light of Life
to that darkness which fosters neglect, pride,
and arrogance. We can lead by example;

the example you gave us; the example of washing
the feet of one another.

Reflection Questions

1. What was your initial reaction to Jesus washing the feet of the disciples? How do you think the disciples reacted? Do you think Peter's initial response to Jesus was understandable? What about his second response?
2. In what ways have you been of service to members of your family, parish, school, and place of work? How did this service help you grow close to Jesus? What forms of service are part of your Lenten spiritual formation?
3. In what ways is the Church called to be of service? What are some of the major forms of service provided by the Church today? How does the Church unite service with sacraments? How does the Eucharist strengthen you for a life of service in imitation of Jesus?

It Was Night

From the beginning of our Lenten journey with Jesus to Jerusalem, we have been alerted to the rejection and hostility that would come. The birth of Jesus greatly troubled King Herod "and all Jerusalem with him" (Mt 2:3). Herod's madness for power caused the Holy Family to flee to Egypt (Mt 2:13) so as to avoid the massacre of the Holy Innocents (Mt 2:16). With the presentation of Jesus at the temple in Jerusalem, the righteous Simeon prophesied, "Behold, this child is destined for the fall and rise of many in Israel, and to be a sign that will be contradicted" (Lk 2:34). The Gospel of John contains in the Prologue what we will find out at the end of the public ministry. "He came to what was his own, but his own people did not accept him" (Jn 1:11). From the mighty who occupied thrones of political power, as well as the religious authorities in the chair of Moses, to those of his home town, Jesus incurred a hostility which gave way to plans for his death. All of this is the work of the world under the influence of Satan. Yet no matter how bad things got, Jesus could withdraw with the Twelve. Away from the world, Jesus could be with those who stood by him in his trials (Lk 22:28). For awhile, the world could be shut out.

The reality of rejection is one thing; the realization of betrayal by one whom Jesus personally called, moves us to a new level of darkness. Yet this is exactly what Jesus will now face. For there is one at the table, one whose feet Jesus has just washed, who will betray him (Ps 41:10; Jn 13:18; 13:21). The dispute over greatness now turns to a general panic as to whom the traitor might be. Denials fill the air. The washing of feet evoked stunned silence; the revelation of betrayal fills the Upper Room with angry voices of protest as they "debate among themselves who among them would do such a deed" (Lk 22:23). Finally, as things spin out of control, the Beloved Disciple ask Jesus, "Master, who is it?" (Jn 13:25).

Jesus does not answer directly, but offers a symbolic response. "It is the one to whom I hand the morsel after I have dipped it" (Jn 13:26). The dipped morsel is offered by the host to a guest of special honor or one who is in need of reconciliation. The dipped morsel is a kind of peace offering in hopes of amending past conflicts. It is offered to Judas, son of Simon the Iscariot (Jn 13:26). However, this is not offered so as to condemn Judas or arouse the other disciples to prevent him from his betrayal. Jesus offers the dipped morsel to Judas as a final gesture to reconciliation. Judas can still turn from what he is about to do. Jesus loves Judas, most especially Judas, because of his great need for love till the very end.

It is not to be. Judas takes the morsel; but, "Satan entered him" (Jn 13:27). Jesus can offer forgiveness and healing, but it is up to each individual to accept or reject the invitation. Judas refuses this final offer by Jesus. In so doing, he freely commits himself to do the work of Satan. After the final temptation of Jesus in the desert, we are told that the devil "departed and waited for an opportune time" (Lk 4:13). This is the most opportune of times. Judas is now doing the very work of Satan. The Prince of Darkness has found an ally in trying to extinguish the Light.

Do Quickly

Jesus knows it is Judas who will hand him over. If only Jesus will alert the others, Judas can be stopped. Jesus can flee and return to the safety of the desert away from Jerusalem. He will not have to endure his rejection and crucifixion. Jesus will also not complete the work given him by the Father.

Jesus ensures a safe passage for Judas. Amidst the general confusion and uncertainty, Jesus dismisses Judas to do quickly what he must do. So Judas leaves. We are told, "And it was night" (Jn 13:30). This was not said to merely inform us about the time. The Fourth Gospel is associating night with darkness. The darkness is the realm of evil where Satan rules. Judas gives in to that realm in order to carry out his betrayal. Judas can no longer remain in the presence of Jesus, the true Light of the World. Judas must seek the darkness because his deeds are evil. Judas has rejected the Light of Life and so must walk into the darkness (Jn 8:12). When Judas enters the night, Jesus says, "Now is the Son of Man glorified, and God is glorified in him" (Jn 13:31). Previously when some Greeks came to see Jesus he proclaimed, "The hour has come for the Son of Man to be glorified" (Jn 12:23). The glorification would take place in a way similar to the grain of wheat, which must die in order to bring forth abundant life. When Judas leaves, the ground is now prepared for Jesus to be received, so that through his death the abundant life will come forth.

The New Commandment

Even with the forces of darkness and death all around, Jesus remains forever the Light of Life. Jesus shines in the darkness, and he is not overcome by it (Jn 1:5). Jesus gives the disciples that alone which conquers the night, namely, the new commandment to "love one another" (Jn 13:34). That alone which overcomes fear, hatred, death, and sin is the power of love. Not just any kind of love, but the love Jesus has for his disciples (Jn 13:34). It is the love which denies oneself and takes up the cross. It is the love which goes into the earth so as to bring forth an abundant harvest of life. It is that love which washes the feet of the disciples. And it is that love which is lifted up on the cross for the world's salvation.

Jesus will not expand the darkness. He offered reconciliation. He even protected the one who has left to betray him. Jesus must now look after those who remain. They must stay with the Light and shun the night. They must love one another in imitation of Jesus. This is their test for discipleship. Showing such a love is our test as well (Jn 13:35).

PRAYER

O Lord, time and again we betray you by
our sins. Yet time and again you call
us back to you. You always offer us the
dipped morsel because we need to be
nourished by your forgiveness. We need
that food for eternal life.

O Lord, too often we find ourselves refusing
your invitation to change. We become
comfortable with our sins. We are afraid of
who we might become. Lord, we often
go with Judas into the night. The light
of your truth is too much for us. However,
you call us back to that life which only
comes from you.

O Lord, you give us a commandment—
love one another. But we are to love
in imitation of you. That is, we are to
love in a way that is sacrificial,
humble, and life-giving. It is through
our love for one another that we
show we are your disciples.

O Lord, let us remain with you, the
True Light which gives life. Keep us
from the darkness of the night. Keep us from
that evil which brings death. Let
us love in word and deed.

Reflection Questions

1. In what ways have you betrayed Jesus? In what ways have you tried to reconcile with Jesus? What motivated you to betray Jesus?

2. Do you find it difficult to accept Jesus' forgiveness? Why? Are you able to forgive yourself? Others? Are you able to accept the forgiveness of others? Does guilt keep you from living your life in a blessed way? How might Jesus free you from the burden of past guilt?

3. In what ways have you imitated the love of Jesus in your daily life? What obstacles keep you from following Jesus' way of life? Have you been able to overcome these with the help of your Lenten spirituality? How?

I Will Lay Down My Life For You

It is hard not to like and identify with Simon Peter. In many ways he reminds us of Everyperson. We can easily see ourselves doing and saying the very things Peter does and says. The Gospel portrait that emerges is one which covers the full range of human highs and lows. He is a fisherman who will be given the keys to the Kingdom of heaven; he is the first disciple called by Jesus and yet often misunderstands the ways of the Kingdom. Peter receives a divine revelation about Jesus as the Messiah and finds himself doing the work of Satan by trying to keep Jesus from Jerusalem. He is present at the Transfiguration but wants to avoid the disfiguration of the cross. Peter walks on water toward Jesus and begins to sink when he realizes where he is, and Simon Peter is invited by Jesus to pray with him in Gethsemane only to fall asleep and leave Jesus alone. In all of these and many other instances, we see a wonderfully human presentation of the man called Peter. One thing is sure; Peter was not lukewarm. He was at the bookends of human emotion when it came to Jesus and life.

The darkness of betrayal does not merely engulf Judas. The night reaches out for the Twelve as a whole. The forces of evil are not satisfied with the son of Simon the Iscariot. The little flock must be "scattered, each going his own way and leaving [Jesus] alone" (Jn 16:32). Indeed, when the cohort comes to arrest Jesus, the disciples flee. The sheep abandon the Good Shepherd. This abandonment of Jesus by the disciples is not merely a human weakness, a failure of courage. The Gospels see the very presence of Satan at work. This evil presence intends on destroying

Jesus and the disciples. Judas has done the work of betrayal. Satan is now looking for one who will complete the task. Satan needs one in the inner circle who will deny Jesus and send the remaining disciples into the night with Judas.

Sift You Like Wheat

Who better to attack than the one who was given the keys to the Kingdom? For if Peter, the rock, can be weakened in his commitment to Jesus, the others will surely deny Jesus as well. Unlike with Judas, money won't work in bringing about the fall of Peter. Satan must look within the man. Beneath the bluster and bravado, there is a fear in Peter that can be exploited. And exploit it Satan will! At the same time, Jesus, ever the Good Shepherd, takes Peter into his prayerful counsel. "Simon, Simon! Satan, you must know, has got his wish to sift you all like wheat; but I have prayed for you, Simon, that your faith may not fail, and once you have recovered, you in your turn must strengthen your brothers" (Lk 22:33). Jesus offered Judas the dipped morsel as a way of staying with the Light, but he refused and went into the night. Jesus prays that Simon (it is interesting that Jesus does not call him Peter, for soon he will not be rock-like in his commitment to the Lord) may ultimately be "delivered from the evil one" (Mt 6:13). For it is clear that Simon will fail in the short term. To his bitter regret, Simon will give a trilogy of denials. "Woman, I do not know him"; "My friend, I am not" (a disciple); and "My friend, I do not know what you are talking about" (Lk 54-65). As the words of denial fill the air, Jesus passes Peter and looks at him. Peter remembers his words of courage—"I will lay down my life for you" (Jn 13:37)—as he now faces the reality of his denials of Jesus. "He went out and began to weep bitterly" (Lk 22:62).

Simon Peter goes into the night. But his journey is not one of despair but contrition. His tears of remorse are an expression of deep sorrow. Yes, he must leave the Light. The look of Jesus is too much to endure at the moment. However, deep in the recesses of Peter's heart is the knowledge that Jesus is forgiving love. Peter has seen the Lord welcome sinners and expel the demons of evil. Peter has heard the parables of divine mercy. Peter has known the wrath of Jesus ("Get behind me Satan"), but he has known the love of the Master even more. And in this moment of denial, no doubt the words of Jesus echo within Peter, "…but I have prayed that your own faith may not fail" (Lk 22:32). There is still hope. Always hope!

STRENGTHEN YOUR BROTHERS

In the words of Saint Paul, "At present we see darkly, as in a mirror, but then face to face" (1 Cor 13:12). We cannot judge the whole of a life on the basis of a single episode. Our lives are not photographs as much as a movie which may surprise at the end. We cannot judge Peter on the basis of his "failed faith," any more than we can judge Peter on the basis of receiving "the keys to the Kingdom." These are parts of the man named Peter (and each man and woman). The whole of our lives will only reach its complete meaning at the end when we see God face to face.

This low moment in Peter's life is real. The Gospels don't cover up his failure. However, we must also remember that Jesus wants Peter to "strengthen your brothers" (Lk 22:32). He will do just that. For the condemned Jesus who looks at Peter in the garden will be the Risen Lord who ask Peter, "Simon, son of John, do you love me?" (Jn 21:15-19). The Simon of the garden denials has become the Peter who can say, "Lord, you know that I love you" (Jn 21:16). In time, Peter will strengthen the Church by that radical following of Jesus through his own martyrdom (Jn 21:18-19).

TURNED BACK

Lent is that grace-filled time of the Lord when we open our hearts to conversion. There is no guarantee that we will stay with the Light of Life. We can, like Judas, refuse the dipped morsel and go into the night. But there is also the example of Simon Peter. The Lord prays that we too might turn from our daily denials and betrayals, so as to strengthen others in the faith. We too may have cause to weep bitterly. The Lord looks at us intently. We must also remember that the look of the Lord is one of forgiveness and not condemnation. At this very moment, Jesus' words are for us: "I have prayed that your own faith may not fail..." (Lk 22:32). There is still hope. Always hope!

PRAYER

O Lord, each day we deny we know you; we deny
we have been in your company; we deny that we
are one of your disciples. We do this by large and
small acts of disregard toward you and our
neighbor. We lack the courage to give witness
to your truth. When we are confronted by the
voices of the world, we grow silent. We claim
that we are just like everyone else.

O Lord, help us to live as your disciples, and
not like everyone else. Help us not to be
conformed to the world, but empower us to transform
that part of the world we touch. Let us
be an instrument of your truth. Let us be a
light which shines into the darkness. Let us
bring your Light of Truth to everyone we meet.

O Lord, we need you to pray for us. Satan
wishes to turn us from you. We will be
sifted as wheat. Let us be that grain of wheat

which falls into the earth so that we might
rise to new life. Let us die to ourselves and sin
so that we may be reborn to strengthen others.
Above all, Lord, let us not give in to the ultimate
temptation of evil—betrayal of you. But let
us join with Peter in that great profession of
faith, "Yes, Lord, you know we love you."

Reflection Questions

1. In what ways have you recently denied being a disciple of Jesus? Did your words or actions influence others? How was their faith weakened? In what ways have you been reconciled to Jesus? To your neighbor? The Church?

2. What was your reaction to the words of Jesus to Peter? Why did Peter deny Jesus? How does Peter differ from Judas? Have you ever lost hope in God's forgiving love? What renewed you in hope?

3. In what ways have you recently affirmed your love for Jesus? Have you been able to inspire others to love Jesus? How? In what ways has Jesus called you to be a source of encouragement to others *after* you had fallen into sin? Were you able to accept the call to strengthen others? How?

How Can We Know The Way?

Throughout the Gospel of John, Jesus has engaged in a number of significant dialogues which eventually become monologues (with Nicodemus, 3:1-21; the Samaritan woman at the well, 4:4-42; the Bread of Life Discourse, 6:22-59; dialogue about the Feast of Tabernacles, 7:1-30; and Jesus as Light of the World, 8:12-20, are all examples of significant teachings by Jesus). These discourses were usually given in a hostile environment before a skeptical questioner. The teaching of Jesus was usually met with unbelief or an imperfect understanding (the Samaritan woman). Perhaps this could be expected. After all, the world is under the rule of Satan and in opposition to Jesus. Often the crowds (and especially the religious authorities) heard but did not understand; they looked but did not see the truth of Jesus (Mt 13:14; Is 6:9-10). With the close of his public ministry, Jesus is now among his own. The disciples are blessed because their eyes see and ears hear what "many prophets and righteous people longed to see... and to hear" (Mt 13:16). Yet we know that seeing and hearing does not guarantee understanding. We may be compared to "children who sit in the market place and call to one another, 'We played the flute for you, but you did not dance, We sang a dirge, but you did not weep'" (Lk 7:31). An underdeveloped faith never sees and hears the truth about Jesus.

TROUBLED HEART

We are no longer in the midst of a hostile audience. We are being allowed to hear the last will and testament of Jesus. The closing discourses of Jesus are given (lasting gifts) to his own who must remain in the world. Jesus will return to the Father. Before he goes, even before the sending of the Paraclete, Jesus opens his heart to those who are his own to the end; those "who stood by [Jesus] in his trials" (Lk 22:28).

The Last Discourse (chapters 14-17 in John) is among the most profound of spiritual writings left to the Christian community. Before Jesus speaks to those at the table (and us as well), he must acknowledge their fear. And the fear is justified. Jesus is about to be handed over to the forces of darkness. He has told the disciples that a traitor is among them. Peter, the leader, will deny Jesus three times. The disciples will be scattered and go into hiding. In the midst of all this fear, Jesus says to them, "Do not let your hearts be troubled" (Jn 14:1). How can he say such a thing?! Of course their hearts are troubled. Yes, they are afraid. Who wouldn't be? Yet Jesus' words remain unchanged—"Do not let your hearts be troubled." Again we must ask. How can Jesus be serious in saying this?

The answer lies with the rest of the quote: "You have faith in God; have faith in me" (Jn 14:1). The courage to face this hour of darkness does not come from our human powers. The ability to remain faithful is beyond our capacity in the face of the forces of evil. Jesus is telling the disciples that the ability to remain faithful comes from a power beyond themselves. The gift of faith will see them through this dark passage. Even more stunning is Jesus' call to place the same faith they have in God in him. Why? Because to see Jesus is to see the Father; to know Jesus is to know the Father (Jn 14:7, 9). The most dramatic of claims is being made by Jesus. Jesus and the Father are *one*! Jesus is God made visible before them. Jesus is God. The call to remain faithful to Jesus is the call to remain faithful to the God who is faithfulness itself (*hesed*). As Yahweh remained faithful throughout Israel's history, now the disciples (the New Israel) are to remain faithful to the new covenant established by the cross (Lk 22:20). In the end, it is faith which triumphs.

The disciples will need a courageous faith to face the departure of Jesus. The real fear of the disciples is the fear of abandonment. They will be left alone to face the hostility of the world. Again, this is a real fear. Once again, Jesus confronts this head on: "I will come back again and take you to myself, so that where I am you also may be" (Jn 14:3). Jesus will never abandon those whom he loves to the end (Jn 13:1). Jesus will show that he is the Good Shepherd by laying down his life for those who follow his voice (Jn 10:14-15). Jesus will not leave them orphans, but he will send the Paraclete (Jn 14:15-18) to dwell within them.

Thomas claims that they want to follow Jesus, but they don't know the way (Jn 14:5). We cannot know the way to Jesus and the Father without acknowledging the truth. And to acknowledge the truth about Jesus, is to enter into eternal life. The way to the Father is through Jesus. In order to be one with Jesus, the disciples must follow the way of the cross. It now becomes clear. There can be no union with Jesus apart from the cross. The truth about Jesus is that he is the Son of God who has been sent to reveal the Father on the cross as SUFFERING, ENDURING LOVE. The faith to follow the way of the cross, and to live the truth of the cross, leads not to death but to eternal life. Hence, Jesus reveals to the disciples, "I am the way and the truth and the life" (Jn 14:6). Throughout the public ministry, Jesus spoke of himself as the way, truth, and life. On Golgotha, Jesus will definitively show he *is* the Way, the Truth, and the Life.

A DWELLING PLACE

Jesus tells the disciples he is going to prepare for them a dwelling place (Jn 14:2). Of course, we think of heaven. Yet there is another dwelling place, the human heart. Jesus has prepared this dwelling place for the coming of the Paraclete. This preparation of the human heart has been going on throughout his public ministry. Here at this final Passover, Jesus washed their feet and called them to a life of humble service. For it is into a heart, a dwelling place, that has been formed by love that the Paraclete will find a home. Is our heart such a dwelling place?

PRAYER

O Lord, our hearts are troubled. We are fearful
as the hour of your crucifixion draws near.
We see the darkness. We know how often we
betray you each day. We too deny we know
you. We give little evidence of being a disciple.
We try to assure everyone we don't know you.

Yet, Lord, you still love us and tell us not to
be troubled. You encourage us to put our
faith in you. We will never be disappointed.
You have never failed us in the past. Your
love surrounds us each day. Your love will
always be with us.

Lord, we want to follow you but we don't know
the way. Yes, Lord, we do know the way. We
find it hard to admit. We know we must follow
you to the cross. You are the true Son of God
who takes away our sins. It is through the
cross that you bring us from death to life.

Each day, Lord, prepare us for the Paraclete
whom you send to dwell in our hearts. You
prepare us for the Paraclete by giving us your
word. You give us an example of humble service.
Let your Paraclete, the Spirit of Truth, come into
our hearts so that we might pass from death to life.

Reflection Questions

1. In what ways have you been spiritually troubled over the past year? How did you respond to the situation? Did you experience the peace of Jesus? How?

2. How have you been able to help others who are spiritually troubled? What was the cause of their spiritual unrest? Did you turn to prayer and the sacraments to bring peace to the troubled soul?

3. How have you prepared your heart to receive the indwelling Paraclete? What obstacles did you encounter? How did your faith in Jesus help you to be open to the call of the Paraclete to live the truth of Jesus?

They Came With Weapons

The arrest of Jesus has all the drama of a Keystone Kops comedy. Led by Judas, a large crowd comprised of soldiers and religious authorities come armed with lanterns, torches, and weapons to seize Jesus and the eleven disciples. Talk about overkill! To further add to this comedy, it is Jesus who goes out and confronts the arresting party. Jesus is so much in control that you begin to wonder who is about to be put on trial. Jesus even instructs the authorities to let his disciples go since they are only looking for him. Jesus cannot resist poking fun at the sight of this huge crowd with all their weapons. "Have you come out as against a robber, with swords and clubs?" (Lk 22:53). Day after day Jesus taught openly and they did not arrest him. Why now? Jesus indicates to the authorities, "this is your hour, the time for the power of darkness" (Lk 22:54). What a "black comedy" we have!

It is really not surprising that Jesus is confronted by such a crowd with all their weapons. The political and religious authorities have been fearful of Jesus from the moment he began preaching. United in their common fear, the authorities turn to what they know best and believe to be most effective—violence. Intimidation, threats, and weapons are the tools of the power of darkness. Yet the comedy of the situation reveals the weakness and impotence of all who rely on such tactics. With fear there is always an exaggeration of the danger, and always an underestimation of the power of truth. The weapons brought against Jesus are powerless to extinguish his power. Torches, lanterns, and swords are no match for the Good News. In fact, those who resort to violence will only help to strengthen the resolve of the persecuted. The blood of the martyrs is the seed of the Church.

The response of the disciples to the crowd is at once understandable, futile, and contrary to the mission of Jesus. The temptation is always there to return violence for violence, weapon for weapon. The result is a culture of death in which the cycle of violence continues through the generations. However, Jesus has taught, "...offer no resistance to one who is evil. When someone strikes you on [your] right cheek, turn the other to him as well" (Mt 5:39). If those who claim to be "children of the light" do not break the cycle of violence, who will? Can the disciples use the methods of the power of evil and not be contaminated? Hardly. Yet the temptation to turn to the sword always appears to be the "realistic" response to violence. But are there ever really enough swords?

The disciples seem to think so. When Jesus tells them about his impending arrest and crucifixion, the disciples tell Jesus they have "two swords." With a mixture of sarcasm and frustration, Jesus tells the disciples, "It is enough" (Lk 22:38). Of course, two swords are no match for the arsenal of weapons at the disposal of the authorities. On a practical level, it is futile to resist. Those who rely on violence always believe their weapons are enough. The resort to violence always blinds its advocates to the futility of mutually assured destruction. Peter, you might know, takes one of the swords and cuts off the right ear of the high priest's servant (Lk 22:50). Once again Peter is rebuked. "Stop, no more of this!" Jesus "touched the servant's ear and healed him" (Lk 22:51). The words and action of Jesus clearly indicate his rejection of violence as the ultimate solution to human conflict. We are not healed by hurting others. The sword does not bring peace. The only lasting victory for peace comes from the One who healed us by his stripes (Is 53:5).

The resort to violence is contrary to the mission of Jesus. That is, to resist the forces of darkness is to avoid drinking the cup of suffering given to Jesus by the Father (Jn 18:11). Violence is simply another temptation by Satan to keep Jesus from being lifted up and drawing everyone to himself (Jn 11:32). To put an end to this hour of darkness would be in reality to extinguish the Light. Jesus will not call upon the "more than twelve legions of angels" the Father would send to rescue him (Mt 26:53). The writings of the prophets must be fulfilled (Mt 26:56).

Left Him And Fled

Jesus, the Good Shepherd, provides for the safe passage of the disciples. However, in reality it is the disciples who leave and flee from the Shepherd. While Jesus loves them to the end, it is the disciples who in the end abandon Jesus. When Jesus first called the disciples they left everything to follow him (Mt 4:20). Now at the end, it is the disciples who leave everything to flee from Jesus. In fact, one of the disciples, when seized by the authorities, runs away naked. In his haste to depart from Jesus, he even leaves his clothes behind (Mk 14:51-52).

All the disciples leave Jesus and flee which comes as no surprise. Jesus foretold this occurrence. "Behold, the hour is coming and has arrived when each of you will be scattered to his own home and you will leave me alone" (Jn 16:32). But Jesus also indicated he would never be totally alone "because the Father is with me" (Jn 16:32). How could it be otherwise, since Jesus and the Father are one (Jn 14:11).

The decision is ours as well. Do we leave everything to follow Jesus or do we leave everything in order to flee from Jesus? Each day, we live our decision.

Prayer

O Lord, we are with you in the Garden and the
forces of darkness surround us. We are afraid.
We are ready to flee. Never mind, we will
stay and fight. We will use our weapons.
We will trade sword for sword. We will
not give an inch. We will meet the enemy
on its own ground and emerge victorious.

Yes, Lord, we know that long ago you
spoke to us of the power of love. You gave
us an example of love overcoming evil.
No, Lord, you have given us an
ongoing example of love's power to
transform and emerge victorious.
Our fears often drive us into the
very destruction we try to avoid.

Lord, help us not to flee. Give us the strength
to remain with you. Let us not turn to
the sword. Let us light the darkness with
your truth and love. In place of the
sword, let us follow your example of healing.
Let us each day say, "enough", enough
with that violence which only destroys.

Lord, we have left everything to follow you. Give
us the courage to continue our journey with
you to Golgotha, and that victory of life over death.

Reflection Questions

1. In what ways have you faced the violence of the world for following Jesus? How did you respond to the presence of worldly violence? How did you overcome the fear which gripped your heart?
2. When faced with violence, do you turn to violence yourself? Why did you not resist evil with the power of nonviolent resistance? How did the situation in which you faced violence turn out? Would you have done things differently? How?
3. Have there been instances when you fled from Jesus out of fear of the actions *and* words of others? What did you think of your actions afterwards? Have you been able to encourage others who face the world's hostility to remain faithful to Jesus? Did this strengthen your own commitment to peace and fidelity to Jesus?

Truth To Power

The demonic dimensions of violence are about to come full cycle in the life of Jesus. Once again, the innocent one is about to be condemned by the guilty; the love of power will seem to triumph over the power of love; and the mighty will inherit tomorrow at the expense of the meek. At the birth of Jesus, King Herod, the chief priests, scribes, and "all Jerusalem" are troubled by the news (Mt 2:3-4). The talk of a Messiah sends them into a panic. God is about to depose the mighty from their thrones and lift up the lowly (Lk 1:52). This cannot be tolerated. The response of the mighty is violence and death. Herod orders "the massacre of all the boys in Bethlehem and its vicinity two years old and under" (Mt 2:16). This mass killing evokes the words of Jeremiah about "Rachel weeping for her children... since they were no more" (Gn 35:19; 48:7; Jr 31:15; Mt 2:18). The echo of her loud lamentation will reach into the Garden of Gethsemane as another of her children is handed over to death. Too much of human history contains gardens with betrayal and killing fields of the innocent who are no more.

Throughout Jesus' public ministry the political and religious authorities, so often divided, were united on one point—Jesus must be silenced! How gleeful they must be at this moment. Jesus, now that the disciples have fled to their homes, is alone with those who have come to arrest him. Jesus will be taken for judgment and condemnation by the forces of darkness whose hour is now.

There is a perennial danger which lurks beneath the surface of every religion, namely, the danger of dogmatism. This corruption of dogma, the essential teachings of a faith, occurs when teachings are closed to any development based on new insights and the ever present Holy Spirit. Religious teachings become ends in themselves and cease being means to the truth about God. Dogmatism becomes a closed system in which those in authority misuse teachings to keep themselves in power and control others.

Throughout his public ministry, Jesus rejected a dogmatism which taught "as doctrines mere human precepts" (Mt 15:9; Is 29:13). Faith becomes a formalistic law rather than the Good News of salvation. Religion becomes a heavy burden rather than a gift of grace which breaks the yoke of sin and death. Jesus did not come to control or bully people into the Kingdom of God. Jesus came out of unbounded love that we might have life in abundance (Jn 10:10).

We see the arrogance of dogmatism when Jesus is brought before Caiaphas the high priest. A number of false witnesses come forward. However, the Sanhedrin is unable to obtain a consistent story so as to charge Jesus. Finally, Caiaphas asks Jesus directly if he is the Messiah (Mt 26:63). How silly! Jesus has been answering this question throughout his public ministry. The authorities hardened their hearts and blinded their eyes then. Why would it be any different now? Of course it wouldn't be. Unbelief persists.

Caiaphas accuses Jesus of blasphemy and says, "What further need have we of witnesses?" Jesus is condemned to death (Mt 26:65-67). The logical conclusion of dogmatism is violence and death. The irony of Caiaphas' work is profound: this is just what every authentic faith needs—witnesses. Not the false witnesses against Jesus, but those witnesses (martyrs) that give true testimony. Jesus is the true witness to the Father. Everyone who believes in him stays in the light of truth. The response of the dogmatist is predictable: "Then they spat in his face and struck him, while some slapped him" (Mt 26:27).

I Have Power

Jesus fares no better before Pilate, the political counterpart to Caiaphas. In a remarkable exchange between Jesus and Pilate, we see the ultimate futility of relying on earthly power. We see the ultimate victory that comes to all who live in the truth.

After some initial verbal sparring, Pilate (ruled by fear) lays his ultimate cards on the table: "Do you not know that I have the power to release you and I have power to crucify you?" (Jn 19:10). It all comes down to power. For Pilate it is the power of the state over life and death. For Jesus it is the ultimate authority from above—the Father. Pilate fails to recognize the limits of the state to effect its will. All worldly power is fading and is legitimate only to the extent that it recognizes the ultimate authority of God. Pilate wants to render everything to Caesar and nothing to God. Pilate lives in fear because the power of the state rests on force and placating the whims of the mob and those in Rome. Jesus lives in freedom because he does the truth in love given by the Father. In reality, it is Pilate who is on trial and found wanting. Jesus is the embodiment of the truth which brings freedom.

Whether before Caiaphas or Pilate, the story line is the same. The real source of strength comes from truth, the blessing of freedom requires the guidance of truth; and, the truth which liberates is the Person about to be crucified (Jn 19:16).

Prayer

O Lord, the hour of darkness grows more
pronounced with each passing day.

The crowds have been silenced for now,
but you find yourself before those
in authority who desire your death.
Yes, the tragedy of rejection by your
own, and the fear of those who rule in
the name of the State is very clear.
Each desires your silence.

Yet Lord, you will not be silent. You came
for truth. You came to tell the world
of the Father's forgiving love. You did
this by healing the sick. You forgave
sin. You raised the dead. Unfortunately,
the response was plotting your death.

O Lord, help us to be a witness of truth
in our daily life. Use us to let your
light shine before the world of darkness.
Use us to speak truth to power. Let
us go forth in your name with love. For
your Gospel is one of truth with love.

O Lord, let us bring the Gospel to others,
not as a heavy burden, but as the
source of hope in turning from sin to grace;
from death to life.
Let us learn from your gentle heart
which brings peace.

Reflection Questions

1. In what ways has your faith given in to dogmatism? Why
   has this happened? What have you been doing to change
   your faith so it is more open to the work of the Holy Spirit?
   What aspects of the Church are in need of reform? Why?
2. In what ways does the State try to control every aspect of

our lives? How can we resist such an all-powerful presence? In what ways has the State tried to control religious freedom? What forms of resistance must the Christian, and the Church, employ?

3. How have you been called upon to speak God's truth to power? Did you suffer because of your willingness to be a witness for truth? Have you experienced opposition from within the Church because of your beliefs? How? How have you responded to the opposition?

Your King Approaches

The response of Caiaphas (and his son-in-law Annas; Jn 18:12-14; 19-24) and Pilate, although they come from different worlds, is the same when it comes to Jesus—violence. Jesus is abused and bound when he comes before Caiaphas (Jn 18-24). Pilate has Jesus scourged, crowned with thorns, clothed in a mocking purple cloak, and struck repeatedly (Jn 19:1-3). However, to Caiaphas, Jesus is a blasphemer who claims to be the Son of God. To Pilate, Jesus is an irritant who claims to be a king of a kingdom not of this world (Jn 18:36). As usual, it is the height of irony that the pagans speak the truth about Jesus, while those who know the Scriptures reject him. It is left to Pilate, the unbeliever, to wrestle with Jesus as the King of the Jews (Jn 18:33, 36-40; 19:3, 14-15, 19). It is this talk of kingship that fills Pilate with such fear. At the most basic level of truth, Pilate knows Jesus to be innocent (Jn 18:38). Yet it is the hard political reality of staying in power that moves Pilate to wash his hands of this innocent man (Jn 19:13).

What a difference a week makes. A few short days ago, Jesus entered Jerusalem amid the expectant cries of the crowd. They spread palm branches and their cloaks along his path. The great crowd went out to meet him. The memory of Jesus' triumphal entry is so fresh that the cries of the crowd still echo in memory.... Pilate fades and is replaced by waving branches.

Throughout the public ministry, and in the final discourses with the disciples, Jesus must often minister to those in the grip of fear. Of course, the story of fear and our humanity extends deep into our history. In fact, the Fall of humankind from paradise cannot be understood apart from fear. Satan plays on our fear, insecurity, and a distorted sense of creatureliness which drives us to grasp for divinity (Gn 3:5-6). The authorities who hear Jesus preach are afraid of a loss of power and status. The disciples fear they have left everything and will gain nothing in return except rejection and death. The sinners and the outcasts live with the constant fear that comes with being judged unworthy and damned. Those who experience physical infirmities fear each new day of pain and suffering. In all of these, Satan finds ways to rebel against the kingdom of God.

The picture of Jesus "riding on an ass, and on a colt, the foal of a beast of burden" (Mt 21:5) recalls the words of the prophet Zechariah. "Fear no more, O daughter Zion; see, your king comes, seated upon the colt of an ass" (Zc 9:9). Into all of the fears which grip the human heart and bloody human history, Jesus comes on an ass's colt with the message—"Fear no more." The triumphal entry of Jesus into the holy city is the victory over fear. Jesus does not come mounting a horse which is the symbol of war for the warrior king. Jesus comes to bring, "Glory to God in the highest and on earth peace to those on whom his favor rests" (Lk 2:14). The first gift of the Risen Jesus to his disciples, followers filled with fear, is peace. "Peace be with you" (Jn 20:19-23). The peace that Jesus brings is not the peace of the world, but that peace which drives out all fear. "Peace I leave with you; my peace I give to you. Not as the world gives do I give it to you. Do not let your hearts be troubled or afraid" (Jn 14:27). Only Jesus can say these words. Only the One who enters the holy city on the ass's colt can bring that peace which endures. It is the priceless gift from the supreme expression of love—the cross.

The triumphal entry into Jerusalem belongs to yesterday, the current reality is standing in the presence of Pilate. Yet it is Pilate who becomes more afraid with each passing moment (Jn 19:8). He is afraid of the crowd which demands that Jesus be crucified. He is afraid of the authorities in Rome who may deem Pilate weak in dealing with rebellion. Above all, Pilate is afraid before Jesus. And in the most profound of ways, it is Pilate who stands in judgment before Jesus.

Jesus did not come to condemn but to save (Jn 3:16). Yes, even Pilate is not outside Jesus' desire to draw everyone to himself. Throughout the interrogation, and often it is Jesus who questions Pilate, he offers Pilate a way to pass from darkness to light. After all, Pilate pronounces Jesus innocent a number of times. Pilate knows the truth in his mind, but he lacks the moral courage to make the just decision to release Jesus. His fear is so intense that he fails to see the source of real power—the truth.

Always it seems the discussion returns to the question of being a king and the reality of power. Jesus tells Pilate directly, "For this I was born and for this I came into the world, to testify to the truth. Everyone who belongs to the truth listens to my voice" (Jn 18:37). The tragedy, not only for Pilate but for Jesus' own people, is the failure to hear the truth which drives out fear. Pilate speaks for many when he asks, "What is truth?" (Jn 18:38).

On this Palm/Passover Sunday, we must ask, Does Pilate speak for us? Or, do we hear the voice of truth who is Jesus the Crucified Christ?

PRAYER

O Lord, you are our King of glory who
comes to us in meekness and truth.
You come to give us the things that are
for our peace. In your kingdom of

truth, justice, and love, there is a
peace which the world cannot give and
cannot take away. It is your gift to us;
help us to receive your gift with
gratitude. Make us instruments of your
peace in our daily lives.

O Lord, we must admit our fears. To stand
before you fills us with a sense of our
own unworthiness. We know our sins.
You look into our hearts and know how
far we are from you. Yet, you say to us,
"Fear no more." How we long to hear these
words. For too long we have been ruled
by fear. We have not known your peace.

Time and again, Lord, you speak to us of peace.
Help us to hear your voice. For your voice
is one of truth. Your truth drives out all
fear because of that love which yields peace.
O Lord, only you can say to us, "Fear no more."
Only you have the power to bestow these words
on us. Give us the grace to not be afraid, so
that we might be yours in all things.

Reflection Questions

1. During this Lenten season, what have been some of your
   main fears? How have you confronted these fears? How
   has God's grace helped you to face your fears?
2. What are some of the major obstacles which have kept you
   from experiencing the peace of Christ? In what ways have
   you tried to overcome these obstacles? How has Jesus
   helped you in your desire for peace? In what ways have
   you been an instrument of God's peace in your daily life?

3. What is your reaction to the encounter between Jesus and Pilate? In what ways have you been afraid of the opinions of others? Did you give in to this pressure or fear? How? How have you been able to resist the judgment of others in order to do what is right?

The Appointed Time

So much of Jesus' time was not his own. He was an itinerant preacher who moved among large crowds with even larger needs. Wherever Jesus went, the word of his coming would cause the sick to go to him in hopes of even touching his garment or having his shadow fall on them for healing (Mk 5:27-29). Others went to hear him preach and teach about the mysteries of the Kingdom of God (Mt 21:10). There were also the constant debates with the religious authorities who questioned Jesus' right to teach (Mt 21:23). Finally, there were many occasions when Jesus had to teach and correct the misconceptions of the disciples (Mt 13:16; 20:20). In all of these instances, someone or some group was always pressing in on Jesus for his time and attention. Jesus' ministry was not scheduled and he did not have the luxury of screening those who came to him. In fact, when the disciples tried to control those who could approach, like the people who brought their infants for Jesus to touch or when they silenced the blind man crying after him, Jesus rebuked such attempts (Lk 18:15; 35). Jesus' ministry was one of service and availability to and for the people.

There is another level at which Jesus had to control his time. This involved the need to remain faithful to "his hour," his "appointed time." With the temptations in the desert, Satan tries to get Jesus to reveal himself as the Son of God before his hour of revelation on the cross (Lk 4:9). At the wedding feast at Cana, Mary makes a request of Jesus before his hour has come (Jn 2:4). And of course there is Simon Peter who does his best to keep Jesus from going to Jerusalem in order to avoid his passion and crucifixion (Mt 16:23). In all of these instances, Jesus had to remain resolute in turning his face to Jerusalem.

PASS FROM THIS WORLD

Jesus' appointed time, his hour, cannot be understood only in terms of his earthly mission. The journey to Jerusalem, and ultimately to the cross on Calvary, is an essential part, but only a part, of the mission given to Jesus by the Father. For even the cross is not a hitching-post but a sign-post. That is, the cross points beyond itself to reveal the glory of the Father shining through the Son. Furthermore, this glory that is revealed on the cross will be shared completely when Jesus returns to the Father. "I have come from the Father and have come into the world. Now I am leaving the world and going back to the Father" (Jn 16:28).

The temptation is great to keep Jesus in our possession, understandable but contrary to the mission of Jesus. Impossible if the Paraclete is to be sent to indwell in the hearts of those who believe, and in the community as a whole (Jn 16:7). Jesus' departure is not a cause for sorrow but for rejoicing. Jesus will be one in glory with the Father, a glory Jesus had with the Father "before the world began" (Jn 17:5). Also, Jesus' return does not leave the disciples orphaned. Jesus will return: not only at the end of the world; he will also return to dwell in their hearts through the Paraclete (Jn 14:18). In a profound way, the world as we know it has come to an end. Judgment has taken place through the cross. It is the world which has been convicted of sin. It is Satan who has been condemned and driven out by the victory of the cross (1 Cor 1:18). Through the indwelling Paraclete who effects the works of love, those who believe have already passed from death to eternal life (1 Jn 3:14). With Jesus' return to the Father, the final judgment has taken place. What remains in human history is the public pronouncement of that one, saving truth: "Jesus is the Son of God" (1 Jn 5:5).

With Jesus' return to the Father and the sending of the Paraclete, the appointed time, the hour, falls to each of us. We are to *continue* the work of Jesus in revealing the Father. We are to continue the work of the cross as SUFFERING, ENDURING LOVE. The true disciple of Jesus is one who lives in fraternal charity towards each member of the community. There is no place for the hatred of one another. To hate, to be a child of Cain, is to be without life. To hate is to be among the living dead (1 Jn 3:11-12). Yet to love as Jesus first loved us is to be born of God. Such a love is not merely with words but with actions. Love is a verb—like truth; it is something we live each day. Jesus' love was expressed in the ultimate revelation of love-in-action, the cross (1 Jn 3:18). Accordingly, "we ought to lay down our lives for one another" (1 Jn 3:16).

The world, that realm of darkness in opposition to Jesus, will not have the last word. The final victory belongs to the One who reigns from the cross: "The message of the cross is foolishness to those who are perishing; but, to us who are being saved, it is the power of God" (1 Cor 1:18). Ours is a shared victory, a triumph of participation in the cross of Christ. But such a victory is only possible through faith in Jesus as the Son of God. "And the victory that conquers the world is our faith" (1 Jn 5:4). We can once again hear the words of Jesus. "Fear no more"; "Do not let your hearts be troubled"; "Take courage"; "Peace I leave with you; my peace I give to you."

PRAYER

O Lord, all of our time is in your hands.
For our time on earth is really your
gift to us. Time is that precious gift in
which we are called to love you and
care for our neighbor. How we use the gift

of time says much about the kind of
person we have become. Let us use our time
to grow in holiness.

O Lord, too much of our time is spent in
idle chatter and gossip instead of
prayer. We talk about others instead of
opening our hearts to you. Help us to grow
in holy silence. Let us use the gift of time
in a prayerful manner each day.

We waste our time absorbed in ourselves. We
fail to see you, Lord, in our everyday lives.
Especially we fail to see you in those whom
we can help each day. Let us think less
of ourselves and more of others. Let us do your
will, Lord, and not our own.

Above all, Lord, let us see our days on earth as
your gift. Let us live each day in gratitude
for all you give us. We do this by surrendering to
you a life of loving service. A life in
which each day we lived toward eternity with you.

Reflection Questions

1. In what ways do you use your time to be of service to others? How much time each day do you spend in prayer? What gifts has God given you that you offer in service to the Church?
2. What are the major priorities in your life? Have these priorities helped you grow closer to Jesus? What major changes in your priorities are you planning to bring about in the future? Where does your relationship with Jesus fit on your list of priorities?
3. Are you comfortable with silence? Do you turn to silent prayer? Do you allow yourself enough rest in order to be

renewed in body *and* spirit? Do you find yourself getting over involved and taking on too many commitments? Why does this happen? How do you plan to give yourself more time for rest and leisure?

The Upper Room

From the multitudes of the heavenly host who sing the praises of God at the birth of the Messiah, to the multitudes who line Jesus' path to Jerusalem, there has been a public, visible dimension to the ministry of Jesus. Discipleship, likewise, involves letting one's light "shine before others, that they may see your good deeds and glorify your heavenly Father" (Mt 5:16). After his arrest, Jesus was questioned by Annas concerning his doctrine and disciples. Jesus responded, "I have spoken publicly to the world. I have always taught in a synagogue or in the temple area where all the Jews gather, and in secret I have said nothing" (Jn 18:20). To be a disciple of Jesus is to be sent out with "authority over unclean spirits to drive them out and to cure every disease and every illness" (Mt 10:1). The disciples are also to go about with the proclamation, "The Kingdom of heaven is at hand" (Mt 10:7).

With the above in mind, it would be easy to assume that the whole of discipleship is found in the visible, public manifestations of the Kingdom. This assumption is wrong. As we find ourselves in Holy Week, we are reminded of the crucial importance of the *hiddenness* of discipleship. The visible and public must be balanced with the need to retreat to an out-of-the-way place for renewal (Mk 6:30). Discipleship requires a time of burial in the earth before the abundant life bursts forth. There is a close to the public ministry when Jesus withdraws to be with his own whom he loves to the end (Jn 12:36; 13:1).

The first day of the Feast of Unleavened Bread, when the Passover lamb is sacrificed, is a special call to the hidden dimensions of discipleship. For the hiddenness of Holy Week is essential for the manifestation of the Risen Lord and the eternal proclamation of the Church: "Why do you seek the living one among the dead? He is not here, but he has been raised" (Lk 24:5).

EAT THE PASSOVER

The Gospels tell us that the last Passover celebrated by Jesus with his disciples is one celebrated in hiddenness. Why? Almost from the beginning, Jesus told the disciples of his passion and death. Again and again, this reality troubled and was rejected by the disciples. They could not accept a Messiah who was also the Suffering Servant. They could not come to terms with a king who ruled from the cross. They could accept the transfiguration but not the disfiguration of Golgotha. The disciples *need* this hidden time with Jesus, during this holy week, so Jesus can plant a final seed in them about *who* he is; and who *they* are to become.

Jesus chooses the ritual celebration of the Passover when the Paschal lamb is *sacrificed*. In the hiddenness of the Upper Room, Jesus will echo the words of John the Baptist spoken long ago: "Behold, the Lamb of God" (Jn 1:36). Jesus is the Lamb of God who takes away sin by his approaching *sacrifice*. Jesus will be the perfect Paschal Lamb who will take our sins upon himself out of love. His perfect sacrifice will be our liberation, our Passover, from death to life; from slavery to freedom; from the bondage of darkness to the liberation of walking in the Light of Life.

If the disciples, if the community of faith and love, are to go forth and "do this in memory of me" (1 Cor 11:24), they must know the hiddenness of the Upper Room with Jesus during Holy Week. Without this sacrificial celebration with Jesus in hiddenness, all their future coming together to remember the Lord would be in vain. To remember the Lord worthily, there must always remain a hiddenness, a mystery, that can only be revealed to those who gather in the Upper Room.

The Upper Room of Holy Week is a place of transit and not a final resting place. Its preparation did not begin during Holy Week. From the beginning, from the first call of the first disciples, the Upper Room was being furnished and made ready. At the River Jordan, two of John's disciples, Andrew and Simon, ask Jesus: "Where are you staying?" (Jn 1:38). Jesus responds with a simple invitation: "Come and see" (Jn 1:39). For the next three years, they will "follow him" to Jerusalem and the Upper Room, to the adulation of the crowd and the intimate setting of the last Passover and first Eucharist, from the shores of the Sea of Galilee to the Upper Room where Jesus washes their feet.

The hiddenness of the Upper Room during Holy Week will pass into that Upper Room where the first community gathered after the Ascension (Ac 1:1-14). The Risen Lord became the ascended Lord. They were now "between the evenings," in the twilight, so to speak, waiting for something to happen. And they were afraid. Once again, they are in the Upper Room. Into that Upper Room of hiddenness and fear comes "from the sky a noise like a strange driving wind" and "there appeared to them as tongues of fire" (Ac 2:1-5). The hiddenness becomes manifest; fear gives way to a bold witness. That day "about three thousand persons were added to their company" (Ac 2:41).

PRAYER

O Lord, you are the Lamb of God who takes
away our sins. Through your sacrifice of
love on the cross, we are liberated from our
true enemies—sin and death. This freedom
comes at a dear price, namely, your dying for
us. But death is not the end. Through your
death and resurrection, we have the hope of eternal life.

O Lord, your Spirit of freedom empowers us
each day to live for you and our neighbor.
Christian freedom is not a call to withdraw
from life. Freedom is not doing whatever
we want, whenever we want. Freedom is the
power to do as we should in imitation of
you. Freedom is being-for-others as much as
we are for ourselves.

O Lord, it is so easy to abuse our freedom.
The desires for self-will and self-promotion
are intense. Too often we think that doing
our thing is your thing. Too often we promote
ourselves with pride and arrogance. Yet your
freedom is guided by truth. We must be
humble if we are to overcome our pride.

O Lord, only your grace can change our hearts.
Only your Spirit can give us true freedom.
Only your love can raise us from death to life.
Only in you do we have the hope of happiness.

Reflection Questions

1. How do you understand freedom? Does your idea of freedom differ from the popular view of freedom as pure self-expression? What difference does it make to add the word "Christian" to your understanding of freedom?
2. In what ways have you been tempted to misuse your freedom? What did you learn about yourself in trying to live freely in a reasonable way?
3. What are your ways for *escaping* from freedom? Do you find yourself blaming others for your failures, sins, and bad decisions? Are you able to forgive yourself when you make mistakes? Do you find it hard to believe that Jesus will forgive your sins? Why?

Without A Disturbance

Our deeds, good and bad, endure long after we die. Too often we think a legacy belongs only to the well known or powerful. Yet each of us leaves our mark on this world. We don't always know the influence we have on others. A word, a gesture, an action which seems quite small can ripple out and affect many in lasting ways. Teachers never know the effects they have on their students. Teachers plant ideas that flower on some distant shore, the fruit to be reaped by others. Parents, clergy, and coaches may seldom hear words of gratitude. However, there are those moments when a child, parishioner, or player returns to acknowledge the gift of long ago: a word of encouragement, forgiveness, and challenge; a sign that one could be better, rise from the ashes, or achieve beyond one's expectations. Even Jesus knew such a moment with the healing of the ten lepers. Only one returned to give thanks for his being made clean. "The man was a Samaritan." What a surprise! The least likely to show gratitude. Jesus deepens his healing of the Samaritan. "Your faith has saved you" (Lk 17:11-19).

Of course, not all legacies are remembered in a positive manner. Some are preserved as reminders of the darkness within the human heart. A special antipathy is reserved for the traitor; for the one who lifts his hand against his leader or comrades, or turns on his intimates. History will forever remember Brutus and Benedict Arnold. History will greatly note and long remember Judas son of Iscariot.

The Gospel of Matthew records the names of the Twelve Apostles. Some contain various marks of identity, either in relation to a family member (Andrew the brother of Simon Peter, James the son of Zebedee and his brother John, and James the son of Alphaeus) or by some past affiliation before their call by Jesus (Matthew the tax collector and Simon the Zealot). When it comes to Judas, he is identified as the son of Iscariot; but also as "the one who was to betray him" (Mt 10:5). That designation will forever be linked to Judas. He will never cease being one of the Twelve Apostles. Likewise, he will never cease being remembered as the one who handed Jesus over to death.

Whenever we face great evil we always ask—why? Why is it that Judas would hand over the One who loved him unconditionally and betray the One who was faithful to the end? The most obvious answer would appear to be money. Even before Judas accepted the thirty pieces of silver from the chief priests, he had a reputation as a thief. Mary anointed Jesus' feet at Bethany with some "very costly ointment." Judas objected saying that the money could have been used for the poor. Yet the Fourth Gospel provides the following evaluation. "He said this, not because he cared about the poor, but because he was a thief; he was in charge of the common fund and used it to help himself to the contributions" (Jn 12:1-8).

Yet we must ask if there was something deeper than money. If we remember, Satan was determined to reveal Jesus' identity before Jerusalem and the crucifixion. Judas was the perfect accomplice. For he wanted Jesus to be a political Messiah who would establish an earthly kingdom. Perhaps a showdown with the authorities would force Jesus to reveal himself and establish his kingdom. Of course, the disciples would sit on thrones judging the tribes of Israel. What Judas did not count on was the resolve of Jesus to do the will of the Father. Jesus would establish his Kingdom, but it would be one of peace brought about by the cross. Judas badly miscalculated the situation. The blood of this innocent man would be spilled.

THE KISS

The contrast between Judas and Jesus is never more pronounced then in the gestures they leave to one another. At the table Jesus knows that Judas has a date with the forces of darkness. Yet Jesus offers him a morsel dipped in the dish as a last offer at reconciliation. By contrast, Judas hands Jesus over with a kiss (Lk 22:47). The very sign of loving friendship becomes perverted by betrayal with the act of Judas. It is Judas who hands Jesus over to be killed, while it is Jesus who effects Judas' escape from the rest of the disciples, "without a disturbance." In the end, Judas gives in to despair and hangs himself (Mt 27:3), while it is Jesus who hangs from the cross as a sign of hope for eternal life (Jn 12:31-32). In the days after Easter, the community remembers Judas as the one who "offered himself as a guide to the men who arrested Jesus," while Jesus is remembered at Pentecost as "a man commended to you by God who went about doing good… God raised him to life…" (Ac 1:15; 2:22; 24).

On this Spy Wednesday when Judas sealed the fate of Jesus, perhaps we should not draw too fine a point on the condemnation of the betrayer. Even the final judgment of Judas is not ours to make. It belongs to the One who is Light and Life. Yes, Judas went into the darkness of the night to do his deeds. However, the Light does shine in the darkness and is not overcome (Jn 1:5). Perhaps, it is into the darkest of darkness that the Light shines brightest. Bright enough even for Judas?

PRAYER

O Lord, often we wonder how Judas could
have betrayed you? After all, he heard

the preaching; he saw the miracles and signs; and he was called by you personally to follow him. How could Judas turn you over for thirty pieces of silver? How could you be betrayed for such a paltry sum?

O Lord, we too hear your word. We too witness the miracles of your grace each day. You call us by name to do your will and reveal the Father as faithful love. Honesty requires, Lord, that we acknowledge our own acts of betrayal each day. In truth, we often betray you for even *less* than thirty pieces of silver. We hand you over to the world for such things as human respect; we are afraid of others; and we want the comfortable life that goes without accepting the cross.

O Lord, we too weep bitterly at our past failure. However, let us not despair. Let us be ever mindful of your mercy and love. You always offer us the grace to return to you. Give us the courage to be faithful and never betray you again. Help us to be faithful as you are faithful to us.

Reflection Questions

1. What is your initial reaction to Judas? What is your reaction to the way in which Jesus responds to Judas' betrayal? What did Jesus teach you about forgiveness and the importance of not being vengeful? Can Jesus' example of forgiveness be used in today's world? How? Can society as a whole learn from Jesus? What lessons?

2. What are the small and large ways you have betrayed Jesus? How have you made reparation for such betrayals? What did your betrayals of Jesus teach you about yourself?
3. Are you able to accept the forgiving love of Jesus? Have you been tempted to despair after betraying Jesus? Why? How did God's grace keep you from despair so as to seek God's mercy? How have you helped others to find God's saving mercy?

A Remembrance Of Me

In these final days and hours between Jesus and his disciples, it would be so easy to lose focus on the things that really matter. Beginning with the triumphal entry into Jerusalem and continuing to this sharing of the Passover, so much has happened. The past several days have been an emotional and spiritual roller coaster: the adulation of the crowds in Jerusalem and the resentment of the authorities; the Greeks requesting to see Jesus and the inability of Jesus to move about in public for fear of arrest by his own people; the voice from the sky proclaiming glory to Jesus and the complete misunderstanding of the "who" and "what" of the revelation; the acknowledgment that many did believe in him while at the same time admitting that even the signs did not move the majority to believe; Jesus' desire to celebrate the Passover, all the while knowing that one would deny and another would betray him; and, finally, the sharing of the bread and cup as the new covenant of love while the disciples are in a dispute over who is the greatest. From this litany, we can easily see how difficult it is to keep focus on what is essential, namely, the Person of Jesus. So often it is the superficial, the banal, and, most of all our own sinfulness, which keeps Jesus from being the main focus of our lives.

Honesty requires that we acknowledge *our* present day lack of focus. As we prepare to celebrate the Last Supper, our focus can easily be diverted from Jesus. We find ourselves involved in the mundane, yet necessary, concerns of everyday life. The challenge is to be involved without becoming absorbed, to care and not to care (T.S. Eliot), to learn that blessed indifference at the heart of Christian freedom (St. Ignatius of Loyola). If we are to be in the world but not of the world, we must *do* the Eucharist in memory of Jesus.

BROKEN AND POURED OUT

An essential aspect of the Christian community is memory. We are a people with a past. We *have* a story into which we are born. We are blessed with the gift of a narrative that saves us from having to make up a new story (identity) each day. We are a people who live the Love Story—not the love story of sentiment, but the sacrificial Love Story of the one who is broken and poured out for the forgiveness of sin.

For the Christian community, memory is not the passive recollection of things long ago, but being present to that which guides our today and helps shape our tomorrow. We celebrate the dangerous memory of Jesus in the Eucharist. Through word, symbol, sign, and gesture we become present to the crucified and risen Lord.

And what is it that we remember? To what, to whom do we become present? In the words of Saint Paul, "Every time you eat this bread and drink this cup, you are proclaiming his death" (1 Cor 11:26). The death of the Lord on Golgotha is the dangerous memory which Satan had tried to derail from the beginning. The temptations are about trying to prevent his death on the cross from taking place. Hence, our remembrance is of his death. We become present to and one with the body that is broken and the blood that is poured out for the remission of sin. The tremendous cost of this tremendous love is remembered and made present for each community. Furthermore, our remembrance of costly love yields a costly grace which strengthens us for the cost of discipleship. We too are to be broken and poured out as a living remembrance of the Crucified One. The Church is the Church to the extent that it proclaims the death of the Lord. Fidelity to such a proclamation ensures the Church must be broken and poured out as well. The Church of the Crucified One stands in solidarity with all those throughout history who incur the hatred of the world.

THE LORD COMES

We are not only a people of memory; we also live within a story of hope. Our memory is alive in the present and helps to shape our tomorrows. If all we have is memory, the community falls into nostalgia and a traditionalism which is closed to the renewing presence of the Holy Spirit. Hence, when we gather to remember the Lord, we also gather to look forward to that end time in which Jesus will commence the eternal banquet. Each Eucharist is a sharing in the bread and wine of that Last Supper. The Eucharist is also a foretaste of that new covenant which we shall share with Jesus at its "fulfillment in the Kingdom of God" (Lk 22:16).

For now, on this Holy Thursday, we find ourselves suspended between the temporal poles of past and future, memory and hope. This Holy Thursday is our time, our present. It is our time of remembrance of the One who was suspended between heaven and earth for our sins. It is our time of hope for the coming of the One who bids us recline at table. Our present task is to celebrate the Eucharist in a worthy manner. That is, we must discern the body (1 Cor 12:27-34). We must labor for that unity of which Jesus prayed before he died (Jn 17:20-21). We must avoid those divisions which fracture the body and give scandal. We must remember and hope in that love which washes feet, is lifted up on the cross, rises from the dead, and, one day will call us home.

PRAYER

O Lord, you invite us to this Last Supper
and First Eucharist on this Holy Thursday
night. You have greatly desired to eat this
meal with us. Yet it is we who should
desire to be with you. It is we who are
greatly in need of a place at table. We
need your word, your example. Above all,
Lord, we need *you*.

O Lord, what we share with you is not only
for tonight but for all of our nights and
days. The Last Supper is a memorial of your
sacrifice of love, and a hope of love's
perfection at that banquet which will never end.

O Lord, let us participate in a worthy manner.
Let us discern your real presence in the
bread we eat and the cup we share. For
you are really our food for eternal life.
We partake of this meal in the hope of being
raised on the last day.

O Lord, let us each day be humble servants to
all whom we meet. Let us wash feet and
be found as those who serve in imitation of
you. For in our loving service, we also
remember you until you come in glory. In
so doing, we partake *now* in your life and love.

Reflection Questions

1. In what ways have you been nourished by the Lord during this past Lenten season? By the Scriptures? By celebrating the Sacraments of Reconciliation and Eucharist? By
various forms of prayer, penance, and service?

2. How has the celebration of the Eucharist been a source of spiritual strength and renewal for you? How have the various forms of service during Lent drawn you closer to Jesus? What particular forms of penance have made you less self-centered and more open to Jesus and your neighbor?

3. How do you plan to *continue* your Lenten spirituality throughout the year? Why are these aspects important to you? What important spiritual insights have you gained over this past Lenten Season?

With Me In Paradise

The Gospel of Saint Luke is one of the most beautiful and best loved of the writings of Scripture. While the Gospel of Mark emphasizes the humanity of Jesus and the cost of discipleship, the Gospel of Matthew is concerned with the fulfillment of the law and prophets by Jesus as Messiah; and the Gospel of John soars to spiritual heights like a eagle; the Gospel of Luke is one that highlights the compassion of God. And this compassionate, healing love of God is made visible in the Person of Jesus. From the beginning of the public ministry, Jesus came to "bring glad tidings to the poor... liberty to captives and recovery of sight to the blind, to let the oppressed go free, and to proclaim a year acceptable to the Lord" (Lk 4:17-19; Is 61:1-2). Throughout the public ministry, Jesus is the Jubilee and Compassion of God. This is powerfully expressed in Jesus' table fellowship with sinners, the outcasts, and foreigners (especially Samaritans—the Parable of the Good Samaritan, Lk 10:29). The parables of Jesus preserved by Luke accentuate the mercy of God (the Lost Sheep, Lk 15:1; the Lost Coin, 15:18; the Prodigal Son, 15:11).

To use, with some modification, the familiar refrain, as it was in the beginning, and throughout his public ministry, so it will now be at the end. From the cross, that text from Isaiah which Jesus read long ago in the synagogue in Nazareth, will come to pass (Lk 4:16). On this Good Friday, the year of the Lord's favor is about to be revealed: a prisoner will be set free.

Death scenes are often romanticized and idealized. The dying person is usually surrounded by family and friends who offer comfort, while waiting to record the last words of the great man or woman. Not so with Jesus. The Gospel states clearly: "When they came to the place called the Skull, they crucified him and the criminals there, one on his right, and one on his left" (Lk 23:33). Jesus dies with those he came to save. There is a deep authenticity about Jesus' death. He is surrounded by those to whom he came to announce the good news. It is fitting that Jesus be counted among the criminals, sinners, outcasts, and despised. Jesus was accused of being all of these himself. Jesus is convicted of blasphemy and leading a revolt against Caesar. He is declared a sinner because he eats with them. Jesus is despised and cast out by the religious leaders who see him as a threat to their power. To find Jesus among the criminals is to be expected.

Once again, as Jesus hangs on a cross with criminals, we hear a familiar ploy: "If you are King of the Jews…" (Lk 23:37). Just before his public ministry, Jesus was tempted by the devil in the desert to reveal himself through some dramatic action (turning stones to bread; jumping off a pinnacle of the temple; and gaining power by worshiping Satan, Lk 4:1). At that time Satan began by saying to Jesus, "If you are the Son of God…"; it is the very phrase used by the soldiers at the foot of the cross (Lk 23:37). This time Jesus will reveal that he is indeed the Son of God and King of the Jews.

And what is the dramatic action which will dispel all doubt about his divinity? Perhaps he will come off the cross and save himself. Maybe he will call on legions of angels to defeat the soldiers. Jesus does none of these. He responds in an even more dramatic and shocking manner: "Father, forgive them; they know not what they do" (Lk 23:34). In this forgiving of the persecutor, Jesus shows the full measure of divine mercy. Jesus does this as only he can—from the cross with supreme love. Because he is the Son of God, Jesus does save, not himself, but all who are open to forgiveness. Because Jesus is the Son of God, he does not come down from the cross but remains there for our sins. Again, the words of Isaiah, "Upon him was the chastisement that makes us whole; by his stripes we were healed" (Is 53:5).

CONDEMNATION TO SALVATION

Criminals and crimes are not to be romanticized. One of the criminals takes up the chant of the soldiers. "Are you not the Messiah? Save yourself and us" (Lk 23:39). The mere fact that one is a criminal and in the presence of Jesus on the cross is no guarantee of conversion. However, Jesus is the Messiah and did come to save the lost and call home those who traveled to a distant land (Lk 15:13). The second criminal, Dismas, is not a romantic but a realist who received a sentence which was just. Once again, it is the criminal who is able to see the truth. "We have been condemned justly, for the sentence we received corresponds to our crimes, but this man has done nothing criminal" (Lk 23:41). It is the sinner and despised who is able to correctly evaluate the situation and give testimony to Jesus: "This man has done nothing criminal."

The final act of the public ministry for Jesus, from the perspective of Luke, is to accept the conversion of Dismas. What Jesus has done throughout his ministry, he will do in this final hour—forgive the unforgiven, and, above all, bring the dead to life (Lk 15:32). In so doing, heaven breaks into song and celebrates the return of the one repentant sinner. The entrance by Dismas into Paradise reveals the work of the Son of God. Here at the end, which is really the beginning, Jesus does reveal who he is—the Jubilee and Compassion of the Father. This is indeed a *Good* Friday.

O Lord, we find ourselves at the foot of the
cross. We know that our sins have added
to your suffering. Our daily denials and
betrayals have added to your stripes and
wounds. Each day we have returned your
love with indifference; your forgiveness
we have failed to share with others; your
kindness we have taken for granted.

O Lord, at the same time as we look up
to you in our sinfulness, you once
again offer us a way into Paradise. It
is not that we deserve your mercy,
but we are so in need of your healing.

O Lord, we have been the arrogant thief
on the cross. We have tested your love
and doubted your capacity to forgive.
We admit our sins. Our faults are
always before us.

O Lord, on this Good Friday, look at us
once again with love. Help us to acknowledge
our failures. Wash us of our sins with
your blood, and by your stripes, heal us.
O Lord, we long to hear those words, "You
will be with me in Paradise."

Reflection Questions

1. Do you find it hard to imagine Jesus showing such great
   forgiveness from the cross? Why? Do you find it hard to
   accept Jesus' forgiveness of your sins? Has this kept you
   from Confession and Eucharist?

2. In what ways have you tested the forgiveness of Jesus? How did the Lord respond to you? Were you able to return to the Lord to accept his mercy? If not, why? If so, what did you experience?
3. Do you ever feel that the Lord will not forgive your offences? Why? Have you been able to overcome these feelings? What turned your despair to hope? How have you been able to encourage others to return to the Lord's mercy?

Laid Him In the Tomb

Few days are as misunderstood and little appreciated as that of Holy Saturday. It finds itself sandwiched between Good Friday and Easter Sunday; a day of profound sorrow and unsurpassed joy; a time of great solemnity and a time of boundless celebration. Holy Saturday carries with it no such extreme. Rather, Holy Saturday seems to be a time of inactivity. It is often seen as a day of transition between the crucifixion and the resurrection. In other words, Holy Saturday has little significance of its own. We even get a head start on Easter with the vigil on Saturday. It's easy to miss the deep theological and spiritual importance of Holy Saturday. To be specific; we can go so far as to say that Holy Saturday accentuates the connection between Good Friday and Easter Sunday, the cross and the empty tomb. Hence, Holy Saturday is not a day of transition but a bridge, a time of connecting the One on the cross with the One who is risen.

The importance of Holy Saturday has not been lost on the Church. An essential component of our profession of faith is, "He descended into hell" (The Apostles' Creed). In the Nicene Creed we profess, "...he suffered, died, and *was buried.*" From the earliest moments of the Church, it was deemed essential to affirm that Jesus was buried *and* he went into hell. The foundation of the Church's creeds saw a clear necessity to affirm the burial of Jesus. There was the necessity of affirming that Jesus descended into the land of the dead "as Savior, proclaiming the Good News to the spirits imprisoned there" (*Catholic Catechism*, 632). Therefore, our reflection on the meaning of Holy Saturday for our Lenten journey with Jesus is not superficial or transitory. Rather, our reflections on this day involve some of the deepest mysteries about the person of Jesus, his mission of salvation, and the consequences of Jesus' death and resurrection for our hope of eternal life.

TAKING THE BODY

It is essential for the victory of salvation that Jesus died a real human death. The Gospels go to great length to assure us of this fact. Jesus "breathed his last" (Mk 15:37); "...Jesus cried out again in a loud voice, and gave up his spirit" (Mt 27:50); "...he breathed his last" (Lk 23:46); and "...bowing his head, he handed over the spirit.... When they came to Jesus and saw that he was already dead... immediately blood and water flowed out" (Jn 19:30; 33; 34). Why make so much over his physical death? Because some of the early heresies held that Jesus never really died our human death. At the time of his death, Jesus, it was said, left and returned to the Father *before* the actual death took place. What was left on the cross was a kind of shell or outer form that appeared to be Jesus. This view taught that Jesus never really died our death.

The Church had to proclaim Jesus as dying our death if sin was to be swallowed up in victory (1 Cor 15:54-56). The wages of sin is death. By Jesus taking on himself our sins and dying our death, he transformed their meaning forever. Sin no longer has the last word. Sin does not emerge victorious with its message of death and despair. Because Jesus, out of total love, took our sins to the cross, the victory is now for life and hope. The Word became flesh (Jn 1:14). The Incarnation was the total acceptance of our humanity by Jesus. There was no holding back. The Father sent the Son completely into our human nature for its healing and redemption. If Jesus had not been fully present in our human death, the victory of sin would continue. In the words of the Apostle Paul, "The sting of death is sin... but thanks be to God who gives us victory through our Lord Jesus Christ" (1 Cor 15:56-57). Salvation comes at a great price. Love demands that Jesus be fully present on the cross. Costly grace demands the full measure of love. Only such a grace can liberate us from sin and give us cause for hope.

A HUGE STONE

The physical, dead body of Jesus is placed in a tomb in which there is "a huge stone across the entrance... fixing a seal to the stone and setting the guard" (Mt 27:60; 66). There is an air of finality about all this. Huge stones, sealing the tomb, and soldiers to make sure no one steals the body carries with it the realization that Jesus of Nazareth has died.

Yet the one who died our human death is also the Christ who draws all to himself. The victory over sin won by Jesus is brought by Christ to those who had fallen asleep. The dead hear the Good News of salvation by Christ. The work of salvation extends to those who are dead. All those, from the earliest times, who awaited deliverance receive the Gospel from the Christ who descends to the dead. An ancient homily for Holy Saturday contains the following: "Today a great silence reigns on the earth.... [T]he King is asleep... and he has raised up all who have slept ever since the world began.... Rise from the dead, for I am the life of the dead."

The huge stone along with soldiers block Jesus' entrance to the world. Yet Christ is active in the work of salvation to all who have fallen asleep in Abraham. Even in the stillness and quiet of the tomb, God is proclaiming the Gospel. Even with soldiers guarding the entrance, the earth will shake and the tomb will give up the One who is Light and Life.

PRAYER

O Lord, we not only fear the cross; in some
ways we find ourselves in greater dread

of the tomb. At least on the cross, there is
still life. The tomb, however, is so silent;
so final. Life is over.

Yet Lord, you enter the tomb and change
its meaning. It is no longer a place of
finality but a sign of hope. Yes we die.
Yes we are laid in the tomb. But
because you went before us, it is now a
holy place. Your presence replaced
our fear with hope.

O Lord, the tomb is a sign of hope
because you will come forth from
the tomb. Your resurrection is our hope
of coming forth as well. We long
for you to call us forth as you did
Lazarus. However, at the call of your
voice, we hope to come forth never to die again.

O Lord, on this Holy Saturday let us be
in the silence of the tomb. It is not a
silence which fills us with fear, but a sacred
quiet that allows us to hear your word
and see your presence. It is a silence of hope
in the life that is about to burst forth.

Reflection Questions

1. What is your reaction to Jesus' being placed in the tomb?
   Does the tomb fill you with dread? Hope? What does Jesus'
   being laid in the tomb mean for your spiritual life?
2. Do you find yourself uncomfortable with silence? Why do
   you find silence helpful to your prayer life? How? When
   you are in silent prayer, are you able to discern the Lord's
   word for your life?

3. Do you visit the graves of your loved ones for commemoration and prayer? How does Jesus' being in the tomb help give you hope about your death and the death of your loved ones? In what ways have you been able to bring hope to those who mourn over a lost loved one? Has the commemoration of Holy Saturday been a source of spiritual strength to you? How?

VI

EASTER AND EMMAUS

Our Lenten journey with Jesus to Jerusalem, a journey from death to life, began of all places with the crib in Bethlehem. We now find ourselves in the company of courageous women (Mary Magdalene, Joanna, and Mary, the mother of James), and "the others" who went along to prepare the body of Jesus. We have been present at the birth of the Messiah with its announcement of peace on earth. Just days ago, we were present at the death of the Messiah on the cross at Golgotha. In place of the heavenly host, we witnessed the earth quaking, rocks splitting, and the tombs of the saints being opened as they rose from the dead (Mt 27:51-52). "From noon onward, darkness came over the whole land until three in the afternoon" (Mt 27:45).

During this Lenten journey of faith, we found ourselves with the Old Adam in the Garden of Eden and the New Adam in the Garden of Gethsemane. We went up Mount Sinai with Moses to receive the Law; we reclined to listen to Jesus, the New Moses, give the New Law of grace with the Sermon on the Mount. We listened to the great prophets pointing to the Promised One. We found ourselves mesmerized at the preaching of "the voice of one crying in the wilderness," John the Baptizer. The Suffering Servant of Yahweh, foretold by Isaiah, was realized in Jesus on the cross.

As we approach the end, which is really a new beginning, memorable phrases fill the mind and echo with the piercing power of truth:

"A Savior has been born for you"
"a sign that will be contradicted"
"Your eyes will be opened and you will be like gods"

"The Lord laid upon him the guilt of us all"
"if you are the Son of God"
"the keys of the Kingdom"
"Get behind me Satan"

"The grain of wheat falls into the earth and dies"
"in your midst as one who serves"
"Blessed is he who comes in the name of the Lord"
"Do quickly"

"Do this in remembrance of me"
"One of you will betray me"
"What is truth?"
"It is finished"

Behind each of these phrases, and countless others, we have witnessed the story of salvation. It has not been an idealized account of God's victory over sin. There has been no attempt to idealize the past or those whom God chooses to do the work of grace. God works through human, all too human, vessels of clay. And throughout these days of Lent, we have had revealed to us the deepest dimensions, good and evil, of human nature. We have had revealed to us the mystery of God's unbounded love.

As we take our leave of Lent and stand on the break of Easter hope, there is the message we long to hear which commences, *not* terminates, our journey with Jesus. It is to these words that we now turn. It is to this commencement address that the remainder of our earthly journey with Jesus finds its direction and truth.

Why Are You Weeping?

There are no eyewitnesses to the resurrection of Jesus. The Gospels tell us that all who came to the place of Jesus' burial on "the first day of the week" found one thing—an empty tomb (Mt 28:6; Mk 16:6; Lk 24:3; Jn 20:2). Each Gospel contains some variations on that first Easter morning, but each Gospel makes it clear that Jesus is not in the tomb. Jesus has been raised from the dead (Mk 28:6-10; Mk 16:6-8; Lk 24:5-6; Jn 20:6-10). He is not to be found among the dead.

The empty tomb by itself does not prove that Jesus rose from the dead. Even Mary of Magdala, who came to minister to the body of Jesus, did not understand the Resurrection. This lack of understanding was also present with Simon Peter and John who raced to the empty tomb (Jn 20:4-10). The empty tomb does not *prove* that Jesus rose, rather, it is an invitation to *faith*. We are invited to look and see with the eye of faith that which is hidden "from the learned and clever" of this world. We are invited to enter the empty tomb with the Beloved Disciple in order to see and believe (Jn 20:8).

If there is one thing which characterizes this first Easter, it is the appearances of the Risen Lord. Easter is a day of appearances. None is more profound and appropriate than the first appearance of the Risen Lord recorded in the Fourth Gospel. The first appearance by Jesus reveals the essence of Easter hope and joy. God continues to surprise us and confound *our* expectations. Throughout his public ministry, Jesus went among the least, last, little, and lost according to the world. Now on the first Easter morning, the Risen Lord appears to one who was once given up for dead but has come back to life (Lk 15:32).

In reflecting on Easter, Saint Paul writes to the Christians at Corinth, "If Christ has not been raised, your faith is vain; you are still in your sins" (1 Cor 15:17). The resurrection is Jesus' victory over sin and death. It is a victory that Jesus shares with all who come to him in spirit and truth. Yet even before the crucifixion and resurrection, Jesus forgave sinners and challenged them to live a new way (Jn 8:1-11). Hence, it is most appropriate that on this first Easter the Risen Lord should appear first to one who was given up for lost but was found by grace.

Jesus, the Risen Lord, appears to Mary of Magdala (Jn 20:11-18). This is the same Mary who was a public sinner and shunned by all the respectable folk. This is the same Mary who met Jesus and was restored to life. Jesus was more interested in her future than her past. Condemnation could not undo what was done; only hope could restore and renew Mary so she could accept the challenge of beginning again.

Mary did not recognize Jesus at first. It was only when the Risen Lord called her by name that she knew it was Jesus. This powerful episode reminds us that Jesus is the Good Shepherd. "The sheep hear his voice, as he calls his own sheep by name.... They recognize his voice.... I am the good shepherd. A good shepherd lays down his life for the sheep" (Jn 10:1-18). Mary hears the voice of Jesus, recognizes him as the Teacher (later she will know him as the Messiah when the Holy Spirit comes at Pentecost), and wants to cling to him. However, Jesus indicates that she has an important work to do.

WE HAVE SEEN THE LORD

Mary is not only called by name, she is also sent by Jesus to do the work of evangelization. "Go to my brothers and tell them, 'I am going to my Father and your Father, to my God and your God' " (Jn 20:17). Mary is to go and tell the disciples the new reality which results from the resurrection and ascension; namely, the disciples who were called "friends" at the Last Supper are now "brothers" to Jesus and one another. Furthermore, they are brothers with the same Father. Because of their faith in Jesus, they have experienced a new birth by which they have "become children of God" (Jn 1:12). This new community, born of faith in the resurrected and ascended Jesus, will go forth to proclaim with love, "We have seen the Lord."

On this Easter, this day of victory, we are reminded of the One who makes all things new. The ultimate power of sin is broken by grace; fear is driven out by love. What the Risen Lord has done for Mary of Magdala, he will do for us. Into our own sinfulness, Jesus comes with that grace that offers us new life. Jesus calls us by name and sends us forth as brothers and sisters united in our common origin—born out of a faith in Jesus Christ (Jn 1:13). *We* are now that community of faith and love which proclaims, "We have seen the Lord." Our weeping has turned to joy. The Easter words of the angels are for us. "Do not be afraid! I know you are seeking Jesus the crucified. He is not here, for he has been raised just as he said" (Mt 28:5-6).

PRAYER

O Lord, the day of our longing has arrived!
With the dawn comes deliverance.
The first rays of light announce the Good News:
The Light of Life is now shining,
never to set again. The Messiah once dead
now lives. The Messiah who went among
the dead now reigns at the right hand of the
Father. It is wonderful to behold.

O Lord, your victory is our hope of glory.
We believe in you. We are your brothers
and sisters born out of a living faith

in you as the Son of God. You who were
crucified are now risen. You who were
laid in the tomb and went among
the dead to announce salvation, LIVE!
And because you live we can face
tomorrow. Because you live we have hope.

O Lord, we are your people sent forth
with a message. "He is risen!" This
Gospel is the hope of the world. It has been
entrusted to us. It is for us to
share with others each day.
We are to tell others of the wonder of
your love. We are to speak of what
your love has done for us. Today, we
pass from death to life.

Reflection Questions

1. Why do you think the Risen Lord first appeared to Mary
   of Magdala? Why didn't Mary recognize Jesus at first? Why
   did Jesus have to call Mary by name?
2. In what ways has the Risen Lord called you by name over
   this past Lenten season? What work did the Lord call you
   to do? How did you respond?
3. How have you been renewed during this Lenten season?
   In what ways are you planning on witnessing to the Risen
   Lord? How will you be able to help others see the Lord?

To Walk Along With Them

The connection of the crib and the cross has been a constant theme throughout our Lenten journey with Jesus to Jerusalem. We face the challenge of *living* Christmas *after* Christmas, and we must learn to find Easter in "ordinary" time. The Christmas story does not end in Bethlehem. The crib became empty as "Jesus advanced in wisdom and age and favor before God and man" (Lk 2:52). Easter does not end with an empty tomb, but the Risen Lord appears to the disciples with the words, "Peace be with you" (Jn 20:19). He sent them forth with the Holy Spirit so that they will be his "witnesses in Jerusalem, throughout Judea and Samaria, and to the ends of the earth" (Ac 1:8). The daily challenge is to find the resurrection in the midst of our many sufferings and deaths. To live Easter in "ordinary" time is to daily die to self so as to be born anew in Christ. In small seemingly insignificant ways, we are to experience the Paschal Mystery, showing a kindness to a stranger; speaking a word of comfort or challenge to another; placing the needs of another over our own; taking the moment of hurt and accepting it with love; standing up for a principle or friend; trying to make an enemy a friend; being faithful to commitments when it is not easy or profitable; and in the thousand and one ways in which we imitate Jesus in being a man and woman for others.

The challenge of experiencing Easter in "ordinary" time is not new to us. From the very beginning, the disciples had to struggle with the Jesus who suffered, died, and rose from the dead. After the crucifixion and burial, the disciples experienced disappointment bordering on despair. One of the most important appearances of the Risen Lord takes place on the road to Emmaus (Lk 24:13). The lessons are enduring and speak to each of us, and the Church as a whole, as we continue to travel our own path to Emmaus... and beyond.

THE STRANGER

Walking is a wonderful way to clear the mind and gain perspective. British philosopher Bertrand Russell used to walk with a note pad to write down ideas as they came to him. When facing a problem in philosophy, Russell would walk in hopes of gaining some insight. With a good walk, the mind and body join together for a wholistic workout.

Two disciples (one named Cleopas who is unfamiliar to us and the second who remains unnamed) are walking toward Emmaus. And disillusionment is walking with them. With each step, the disappointment over Jesus grows more intense. A new walking companion joins their journey, a Stranger who seems to be clueless about the events of the past few days. He doesn't seem to know anything about the death of Jesus at the hands of religious and political authorities. Even more to the point, the disciples "were hoping that he would be the one to redeem Israel; and besides all this, it is now the third day since this took place" (Lk 24:21). Other than the report of an empty tomb and visions of angels by women, no one saw Jesus (Lk 24:24).

And they still have not recognized him as the Stranger in their midst. This Stranger shifts from being a passive recipient of news to one who actively instructs the disciples about the Messiah: "Oh, how foolish you are! How slow of heart to believe all that the prophets spoke! Was it not necessary that the Messiah should suffer these things and enter into his glory?" (Lk 24:25-27). This Stranger goes on to give them a crash course in the Scriptures. "Beginning with Moses and all the prophets, he interpreted to them what referred to him in all the Scriptures" (Lk 24:27).

Even after all this, the Stranger still remains a Stranger. However, below the surface grace is at work. The disciples invite this Stranger to "Stay with us, for it is nearly evening and the day is almost over" (Lk 24:29).

Breaking Of The Bread

A familiar scene emerges. These disciples and Jesus are at table for an evening meal, or so it would seem. This Stranger is acting in an even more direct manner than when he explained the Scriptures to them. This Stranger "took bread, said the blessing, broke it, and gave it to them" (Lk 24:30). With this dramatic action, one so familiar to them, "their eyes were opened and they recognized him, but he vanished from their sight" (Lk 24:31). Upon reflection, they began to remember how their "hearts were burning" when this Stranger, who is Jesus, opened the Scriptures for them. They did not understand immediately what was being said and by whom. It took time. It required reflection with each other. The disciples went to be with the eleven in Jerusalem to give their testimony. What is crucial is their experience of knowing Jesus "in the breaking of the bread" (Lk 24:35).

The grace for living Easter in "ordinary" time is nourished in the Eucharist. When we break open the Scriptures at the Liturgy of the Word, our hearts should burn with love for the Messiah. The breaking open of the Word passes into the breaking of the bread and the sharing of the cup so our eyes are opened to see Jesus. And isn't that what living Easter in "ordinary" time is all about? Aren't we being nourished at the table so we can have our eyes opened to see Jesus? And when our hearts are aflame and our eyes opened to see him, we come to realize there is no "ordinary" time. For each moment is redeemed in the Eternal Easter of Jesus the Christ.

PRAYER

O Lord, help us each day to experience Easter
in the ordinary; in the everydayness of our
lives and in the mundane events that contain
opportunities for grace. Let us see the
familiar we take for granted with new eyes.
Let us love anew so that we may
help transform that part of the world we
touch each day.

O Lord, give us the Holy Spirit that our hearts may
be on fire with love for you. Let your Holy
Word be the foundation of our lives. Let the
Scriptures nourish us in that wisdom
and truth by which we proclaim you as Savior.
O Lord, open our eyes each time we celebrate
the Eucharist. Remove the blindness that
keeps us from seeing you in all things, and
in each person we meet. Renew us so
that each ordinary day may be a grace for
the extraordinary. In the various crosses
we carry, let the burden become a blessing.
Give us the grace to help others with their
crosses.

O Lord, each day we journey in our own
way toward Emmaus. Into our midst come
many strangers. Open our eyes so that we
may see that they are your hidden presence.
In so doing, we journey toward our home with you.

ST PAULS

This book was designed and published by St. Pauls/ Alba House, the publishing arm of the Society of St. Paul, an international religious congregation of priests and brothers dedicated to serving the Church through the communications media. For information regarding this and associated ministries of the Pauline Family of Congregations, write to the Vocation Director, Society of St. Paul, 7050 Pinehurst, Dearborn, Michigan 48126. Phone (313) 582-3798 or check our internet site, www.albahouse.org